Barbara Whitehead was intrigued as a child by the stories of past days told to her by older members of the family, and in her teens began to note down this information. In 1962 she joined the Society of Genealogists and in 1972 began to teach evening classes in Family History. She has taught many beginners, in classes run by the W.E.A. and the Local Authority, and York Family History Society was formed from a nucleus of her students.

The careful methods of research which she learnt while tracing her ancestors have stood her in good stead when doing the preparatory work for her historical novels.

Best Wishes from
Barbara Whitehead

D1421589

Dig up your Family Tree

A Beginner's Guide

to Records since 1837.

BARBARA WHITEHEAD

SPHERE BOOKS LIMITED

First published in Great Britain by
Sphere Books Ltd 1986
27 Wrights Lane, London W8 5TZ
Reprinted 1986
Copyright © 1986 Barbara Whitehead
Graphics © 1986 Linda Haywood

Set in 10 on 11pt Linotron Century Schoolbook

Printed and bound in Great Britain by
Cox & Wyman Ltd, Reading

Addresses and details given in this book are correct to the best of our belief at the time of going to press but are liable to change. Please check before making a journey.

CONTENTS

BEGINNING YOUR JOURNEY

When tracing your ancestors you are setting off on a journey into the unknown past. There is no reason why most people should not be able to make such a journey: although every family is unique the same basic means can be used to trace all of them.

It should be fairly easy to discover your ancestors' history for the last five or six generations, back to the beginning of the nineteenth century, using the records explained in this book. (One of the most important series of records began in 1837 and continues up to today, which is why 1837 was chosen as a place at which to stop.) Some people may be able to find out their family history very easily; others not. Patience and diligence, knowing where to look and what you may expect to find will help you above all. The last hundred and fifty years have been perhaps the most exciting ever; the relatively simple lives of our ancestors were changed by the industrial revolution, to become the highly complex lives we lead today.

As long as you are enjoying your 'voyage of discovery', there are no rules about which part of your family you should tackle. The only rule is to stick to truth and accuracy. You can work out a family tree you can be proud of – black sheep and all! A family where no one had ever put a foot wrong would be boring indeed – and so unlikely as to be impossible!

Many men are interested only in the direct male line, while many women wish to follow back the direct female line. (The female line is much harder to trace simply because of the constant changes of name.) Others may wish to find out if they really are related to a certain famous person; or, what *was* it precisely that Great-grandad did?

You do not need much special equipment, but you do need a special attitude of mind – a detective attitude, for ordinary things can suddenly become important clues. The lives of your ancestors have left records behind them, not to enable you to trace their history, but just as we are leaving similar records today. Family history is much more exciting than any Agatha Christie!

Perhaps the most useful item to buy to begin with is a looseleaf notebook such as a ring binder. You can fill this as necessary with lined pages on which to write notes, clear pockets in which to slide photographs and documents, and plain pages on which to draw out tentative family trees. Right from the beginning you can create a working notebook which is also interesting for other members of the family to look at. Your ambition may be to build up a table of names and dates which can eventually be written out beautifully and hung on the wall, and that is fine – but most family historians want to know more. They want to see each personal life as a whole and also as part of a picture; to know where people lived and what they did and discover or guess at what kind of people they were.

Another thing to have is a stock of stamped addressed envelopes. You are going to be writing to all kinds of people and it is always best to include an s.a.e. If you are writing to a relative, perhaps elderly, or perhaps one you have never met, or to a Record Office to ask what the opening times are, or for any other family tracing reason, you will receive more replies more quickly if you give people the convenience of that s.a.e.

Also buy a 4B pencil. This is for writing notes on the margin of old family letters, perhaps identifying some reference in them or saying where you found them, and for the back of photographs, identifying the people in them. A very soft pencil like this will do the minimum of damage to your precious evidence.

What do you already know about your family? Unless we know where we are we cannot decide where to go. You might think you know nothing at all, or you may know a great deal. In any case it helps to put what you know down on paper. At the very least you know a good deal about yourself!

Oral History

Write down whatever other members of the family can tell you. This is called Oral History (or Asking Granny). Obviously the oldest members of the family will remember farthest back, but don't ignore the younger ones – they may remember something they were once told which nobody else remembers, or, if they are cousins, some evidence or knowledge may have been passed down in their line which is no longer in yours. In any case it is a good idea to let *all* the family know what you are doing. They may come up with bits of information you never suspected. They may like to help. If they remember something they will tell you. If they are about to throw away old photographs or old documents they may give them to you instead. On the other hand they might say that they threw all the old rubbish out last week. That's why it is important to let people know what you are doing as soon as possible.

Whether it seems important or not, write down *everything* that people tell you about the family. You may think you will remember without writing it down which school Auntie went to or what job Uncle Bert did, but you are more likely in a month's time not to feel quite sure. Even if at the moment it is a different branch of the family which interests you, in a few years you may discover that the bit of information you did not bother to write down is the very bit you need for what interests you *then*.

When having a conversation with an old member of

the family you might like to use a tape recorder instead of writing, after which you can transcribe the tape. This is fine if people don't mind having the tape recorder running. It may inhibit some people. Often it is best to concentrate hard during the conversation, then to make an excuse to leave the room for a minute, and jot some notes down quickly so that you can write a proper account when you get home. DO go back to people, ask questions to clarify what they told you, tell them about what you are finding out in other ways. It is surprising how often when you tell people of some little discovery you have made, they say, 'Oh, *I* could have told you that,' which is annoying – but then they go on to give you some extra information. In any case they like to be kept in touch. Usually people enjoy telling you about their early lives and about the family, and you may discover a tremendous amount.

Try to pin people down to dates and places. One person told me he knew nothing about the history of the family. 'You could tell me where and when you were married,' I remarked. 'Of course,' he said indignantly. Using that as a basis, asking whether family events happened before or after he was married, I eventually built up a picture of his early life: the school he had gone to, the street where he had lived, the occupations of his uncles, the fact that the licencee of a certain pub was said to be a cousin, the friend who had worked in a certain factory, the time he learned to swim by falling fully clothed into the river – a host of things which built up an interesting picture, and, as he had lived for some years with his grandparents, details about them which I could never have found elsewhere. Starting from that one date and place, we established in one winter's afternoon by the fire a sound foundation for a family history.

Guilty Secrets

It may be that your family are not co-operative and in fact do not wish you to trace your ancestors. 'You don't

4

know what you might find,' they say darkly. You can of course trace your family without their help. Many people have no living relatives to tell them anything. But it is a pity. The rest of the family are missing out on a lot of fun if you don't involve them.

Usually when people don't want you to look, there is something they don't want you to find. The most frequent guilty secret is a baby who was born too soon – either before its parents were married, or immediately after, or perhaps its parents were never married at all. There were more illegitimate babies born in the Victorian period than at any time until very recent years. It is so rare as to be almost unknown to find a family without an illegitimate or suspiciously early baby in it somewhere. It is said that up to sixty per cent of mid-Victorian brides were pregnant when they walked to the altar.

If it is going to upset you, don't look. If one of your relatives is going to be really distressed about it, don't discuss it with them. One day they will realise that you must have found out by now and perhaps the old shame and self-consciousness will at last be soothed. There are other things which may make your relatives try to persuade you not to search, but these baby problems are the most usual. You must be prepared for anything and view the misdeeds of your ancestors – if you find any misdeeds – as adding interest to the record. People tend to be more fascinated by the odd sheepstealer than by half-a-dozen upright citizens.

Apart from collecting and writing down all the 'oral history' you can from your family, ask if there still exists any tangible evidence of the past. This evidence may be of many kinds. Army medals, family letters, a baptism certificate, a memorial card, the brass plate on a presentation clock, a sampler on the wall, a gravestone in the churchyard. Anything and everything surviving may furnish you with clues and with the very flavour of life in times past. A book from the period of austerity during and after the 1939–45 war, showing the amount of household goods a bride was allowed to buy on her marriage, with her maiden name deleted and her new name written in, is, for instance, a very useful record as well as being interesting.

There is one thing you should start to do right away, and get into the habit of doing; that is, to note down the source and date of information. Begin to do so at the beginning, and make the habit so engrained that you automatically note source and date – both the date you made the note and (later on) the date of the source material. For instance, Aunt Annie may show you a newspaper cutting about a member of the family. The date at the top of your notes will remind you of when you paid your aunt the visit; the date of the newspaper will enable you to find that information again if the original cutting is destroyed. The name of the news-paper would also help. Quite possibly neither name nor date will be on that scrap of newsprint, but if they are, write them down. It might also be possible to borrow and photocopy the cutting.

Drawing Out a Family Tree

Begin straight away to draw a family tree. There are many ways to do this; the essential thing to remember is that family trees are *diagrams of relationships*, in the same way that the maps of the London Under-ground are diagrams of the Tube system, and not actual pictures of it. If a family tree is a diagram, then it can represent those real beings, your ancestors, in different ways, telling us different things about them.

When two people marry the union between them is most often symbolised by an equals sign, = , as in

$$John \; = \; Mary$$
$$Green \qquad Brown$$

It is often also symbolised by a small *m*.

A child of this union is shown as coming from it like this:

$$John \; = \; Mary$$
$$Green \quad | \quad Brown$$

$$Ann$$
$$Green$$

just as a child draws its genetic inheritance equally from both parents. If there is more than one child of the union they are shown like this:

7

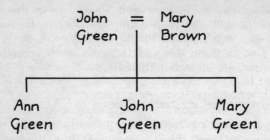

If Mary died and John married again you would show it like this:

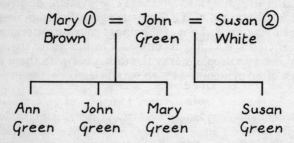

Nowadays, when so many divorces take place, second and third marriages can be shown in this way. Marriages used often to be ended by the very early death of one of the partners and it is quite common to find that one of our ancestors married two, three or more times, and this could happen remarkably quickly. I heard of one case where a lady was married three times within thirteen months. She went out to India with her soldier husband – he died, leaving her stranded out there with a small child. She married another soldier in the regiment – he died; she then married again. This marriage lasted for the rest of her quite long life. Often, when a wife died in childbed, the widower, left with small children and no obliging sister or mother to take care of them, would marry again in a few months. Nowadays divorce is a more common cause of multiple marriages. It can be difficult to show the several marriages of one person in your family tree, particularly when there are children from each partnership. You will probably have to try again and again before you are satisfied with the clarity of your diagram.

Just as you show the children of a marriage so you can show the parents of the husband and wife:

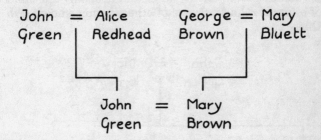

Obviously, before long your family tree is going to be growing wildly in all directions if you try to include everybody, cousins and uncles and aunts. It is a good idea to draw out your first rough attempts on the back of left-over pieces of wallpaper. In fact, there are few better things for family trees; left-over bits of wallpaper (smooth, not embossed, of course) are free and surprisingly strong and durable. You can roll them up and stand them in a corner or sit them on top of a wardrobe or in an old suitcase. Then, when you draw out your lovely neat tree showing just what you wish to show on it, the big rough untidy tree is still there for you to refer to for fuller information – it might include all the more distant people who had to be missed out for the sake of clarity in your best copy, and odd notes you made on the edges as you went along.

On the neat tree you might decide that there is only

room for one family name, and you can indicate what is missed out like this:

John   =   Mary
Green   Brown
             (For Brown family,
             see separate tree)

If you have room for the descendants of only one child of a family, the existence of others can be shown like this:

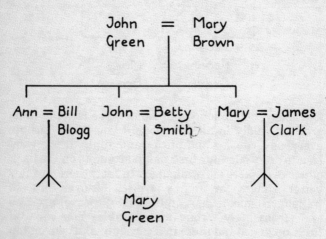

You have shown that although both Ann and Mary had children, on this particular tree you are only showing details of the child of John Green junior and his wife.

At one time it was usual to show all the sons of a marriage on the left-hand side of the pedigree and all the daughters on the right. This seems to be an outmoded convention. It gives you a much better idea of the family if the children are shown in the order of their births, with the oldest on the left and the youngest on the right. A person's position in the family makes a lot of difference to them. Being the responsible eldest is not at all like being the petted baby of the family, and being the only son with seven younger sisters is not at all like being the only son with seven older sisters.

To show an illegitimate child, use a wavy line. If you want to put in a relationship which you think is correct but you are not yet sure of, use a dotted line.

Another kind of tree is known as a Birth Brief. It shows the people from whom you are actually des-

1 YOUR DETAILS	2 YOUR FATHER'S DETAILS	4 YOUR FATHER'S PARENTS' DETAILS
	Name	
	Born	
	At	
Name	Died	5
	At	
Born	Married	
	At	
At		
Married	3 YOUR MOTHER'S DETAILS	6 YOUR MOTHER'S PARENTS' DETAILS
At	Name	
	Born	
Spouse	At	
	Died	7
	At	

Birth Brief

cended and no one else. (It is in exactly the same format as the pedigrees of dogs and cats.) It is built up as in the chart on p. 11.

The next column in the chart would show your great-grandparents, and you can extend it in this way to show further generations. If you join a Family History Society, you are often given a Birth Brief form and asked to hand it in when you have completed it. Do not worry if you can't fill it in. It takes many people years to find the information to fill in a Birth Brief and anyway you might not *wish* to find out all the information required. Most people, though, do enjoy filling them in and the first generations at least are not too difficult. It is quite an achievement to be able to say that you have identified your sixteen great-great-grandparents. Some people become so enthusiastic that they want to go on to discover their thirty-two great-great-greats and their sixty-four great-great-great-greats and . . .

In this book you will find sections about family heirlooms which you may come across, like photographs and postcards; sections with examples of other people's research and what they discovered; and great long sections about the places you might visit to find information, and what you might find there.

It is a 'nuts and bolts' book. It is to give you the essential information to trace your ancestors for yourself, back to that important date, 1837. The magic, the mystery, the excitement, the dull patches when nothing is found, the thrill when something is found at last – that is for you to discover, that is for you to experience.

MEMORABILIA

There are many different kinds of things you may find, kept by someone in the family – samplers, apprenticeship papers, school reports, War service records, and much more. The illustration on p. 14 shows the wonderful personal details given by Army Discharge Papers, if you are lucky enough to have some in the family.

Family Bibles

One of the things you may discover in your family is an old family Bible. Often in Victorian days a young couple would be given a large Bible when they were married, and on the blank leaves they would proudly write their names and the date of their marriage, and then enter the names of the children as they came along, together with any other relevant information they wanted to record.

Even if you think there isn't one in your family, keep asking. Eventually I discovered two in mine, both now in the care of distant cousins, one for my mother's family and one for my father's. By the time they turned up I already had the information they contained, but a photocopy of each is a very nice addition to my family history records.

Usually family Bibles show only one set of parents and children; they are usually mid- or late nineteenth century, or early twentieth century.

Postcards

Many families have postcard albums or loose postcards, and these can be very helpful. Not only for the

PARCHMENT CERTIFICATE of Discharge of No. *4802* (Rank) *L⁰ Sergeant*

(Name) *Joseph Wilson*

Bn. *Middlesex* Regiment.

Born in the Parish of *Boston* near the Town of *Boston*

in the County of *Lincolnshire*

Attested at *Hounslow* on the *6th March* 18*96*

for the *Middlesex* Regiment, at the Age of *20½* years.

He is discharged in consequence of *the termination of his first period of engagement*

Service towards completion of limited engagement	Army *7* yrs., *0* dys.	Medals and Decorations	*Queens South African t6 Class. King S. African t2 class. 2ⁿᵈ Class Certificate of Education.*
	Reserve *5* yrs., *0* dys.		
	Total *12* yrs., — dys.		

* Service Abroad *3* yrs. *235* dys.

(Place) *Hounslow*

(Date) *5th March 1908*

(Signature of Commanding Officer) *Brinsley, Colonel J/c Records, No 10 District*

Discharge confirmed at *Hounslow*

Signature *Brinsley Colonel J/c Records, No 10 District*

Date *5th March 1908*

* To be left blank for completion by the confirming authority.

messages on the back, and the addresses to which they were sent, but also for the pictures on the front. Between 1900 and 1918 millions of postcards were produced of every conceivable place; even if your ancestors lived in a tiny hamlet there is probably a postcard of it, perhaps including their home or even themselves. (Family photographs were also often reproduced on postcards).

Miss K Hopkins
42 Hopkins 200??
42 pr ?? Battgy =
Happy [illegible]

My Dear Fred thanks
for P.C. it is a
nice one. I hope you are
Well, you did not say
we are all well at
present moment doe
not get any better
yet, Dear till you
might come oke your
old Post cards so I have
got a Album and its
empty so I want
you to do one with
me do you get more
they do hone with
your loving Aunt Cath
[illegible]

The postmark, if it is legible, will tell you the place and the date of posting; the value of the stamp will help too – up to 1918 postage was a halfpenny. A reverse side divided into two sections, one for message and one for address, was allowed in Britain after 1902. If a photograph has been enlarged to postcard size and printed as a postcard, with provision for messages on the back, it is likely to date between 1902 and 1920.

Naturally, a postcard might be kept for a number of years before it is used, so the one set of information – from the back – may be of a different date to the other kind of information from the front. The names of shopkeepers may help to date a scene, also the clothes worn by any people in the picture, and so on.

Photographs

The earliest photographs you are likely to find of your ancestors are:

Daguerreotypes, (*1839–c.1857*) and *Ambrotypes,* (*1852–1863*)

These are usually in charming cases and are rather similar to one another in appearance, though Daguerreotypes have a mirror-like look which Ambrotypes do not have. Ambrotypes may have a little hand-tinting, in colour. Treat them with care and do not try to restore them unless you are expert in photography and know what you are doing. If you do not know who the people are in these photographs, the relatively short period that they were in use may help you to make an intelligent guess. Sizes range from one and a half inches by one and three-quarters, to eight and a half by thirteen inches, though the most common size is two and three-quarters by three and a quarter.

Calotypes, (*1841–1857*)

These are much rarer and you are not very likely to

find them. They are in the form of paper prints with no gloss and a reddish-brown colour.

Tintypes, (1856–1938)
Early specimens of these may be cased like the more attractive Daguerreotypes and Ambrotypes, in which case you might not be able to tell what the process was unless you take it apart, which seems drastic. The process survived as a rapid way of taking photographs in places such as fairs. The colouring tends to be grey.

Cartes-de-Visite, (1859–1914)
These are the old photographs most commonly found, and were so popular that once they were invented they must have almost superseded the other types. They are mounted on card backings and usually the name of the photographer and the town he worked in are on the back, or on the bottom border at the front. The size is about two and a half inches by four inches, and the colour is pale sepia, unless 'toners' have been used. Once Cartes-de-Visite came in, *everybody* got themselves photographed, and they were often printed in sets of four. Your main problem, if no one can help you identify them, will be to find out who the photographs are of.

Cabinet cards, (1866–1914)
These were a larger version of the Cartes-de-Visite, measuring about four and a quarter by six and a half inches.

Glass negatives
Once these came into use, around 1878, the amateur photographer was able to get in on the act and they continued to be used up to the early thirties. The obvious problem with these is their fragility and it is wise to re-photograph them as soon as you can.

Flexible film

This came in 1889 but had a nitro-cellulose base which decays. If you find any of this early type re-photograph them without delay. Film as we know it today began to be used during the nineteen-thirties.

Amateur 'snap-shots' came in about the 1890s; both Kodak and Box Brownie cameras were available for use by 1900. This does not mean that everybody had one, as is the case today. Ordinary people could not afford such a hobby until much later, and the studio photograph still reigned supreme.

Later photographs can be amazingly difficult to date. Apart from hand tinting, which was still done on a large scale in the late nineteen-forties, most photographs were in black and white until less than forty years ago, when colour film began to be more available. It is only during the last twenty years that non-professionals have taken many colour photographs.

As colour film is said to have a life of only twenty years before fading, it is best to take copy-photographs of your heirloom prints in black and white.

It helps to show old photographs round the family. Some enthusiastic photographers make blow-up slides of old family pictures and then give a party to which they invite all their relatives (particularly the older ones) and have naming sessions, in which all kinds of interesting information comes out. Try to find out Who, What, When and Where.

Now that copying photographs is fairly cheap and easy it makes good sense to copy or have copies made of the most important photographs in the family collection and to distribute them. Relatives are often willing to lend photographs for the purpose of copying or to have them copied for you. If you have several copies around the family they are more likely to survive for the enjoyment of future generations. The posed studio photograph is not always the one we most prize today – the snap of Great-grandfather shearing a sheep or standing by an early automobile may be much more fascinating.

Old photographs may be dusted with something very delicate, such as an artist's soft water-colour brush, and if you can identify the people, you can write their names with a soft pencil on the back, very lightly and near the edge.

Old negatives should be handled as little as possible and *never* written on with *anything*. They can be dusted with a soft water-colour brush, but advice on the best way to treat them should be sought as soon as possible.

If there is a newspaper cutting or scrap of paper with writing on among the photographs it may give valuable information about them. Even old decayed wrappings of newspaper should not be thrown away without being looked at carefully. Note down the dates and anything which may be of interest.

People were usually photographed in their best clothes, and fashion is a good pointer to date. For men, top hats tend to appear between 1845 and 1875; bowler hats were prevalent between 1885 and 1915.

It is a good idea to think of your own new photographs as part of the continuing record of your family. If you don't do it already, begin the habit of writing on the back edge Who, What, When and Where. Even after a few years it is often hard to remember which year you holidayed in which place.

Preserving old photographs deserves a specialist section to itself, but briefly, take copies when you can; use metal frames if you are framing photographs; see that the glass does not come into contact with the surface of the print, and frame a copy rather than the original; never hang photographs in sunny places; do *not* use plastic-paged albums; avoid all plastics and modern glues.

The best way of storing your original prints is in an

acid-free box (the firm of Ryder in Milton Keynes make them). Mount the photographs on acid-free archival paper by putting their corners through slits in the paper. Or place them in acid-free paper envelopes. Archival paper can be bought from Ryder's or from Atlantis in London, who also have acid-free paper envelopes. The box of photographs should then be kept in a stable low-humidity environment away from extremes of temperatures – an airy shelf in a bedroom would perhaps be the best sort of place. Make a list so that you can find the photographs quickly.

For clear pockets for photographs, use those made by Secol of Thetford, Norfolk.

If your new or copy photographs are to be an heirloom in themselves, they should be printed on fibre-based paper; buy this from Kodak or Ilford.

Books to read on photographs

A good book with clear instructions on copying, preserving, etc. your family photographs is *Shoots, a guide to Your Family's Photographic Heritage*, by Thomas L Davies, published in America by Addison House, Danbury, New Hampshire.

If you cannot get hold of this, you should be able to find *Family History in Focus*, edited by Don Steel and Lawrence Taylor and published by Lutterworth Press in 1984. This is also very good; Chapter 4, on identification and dating of costume, by Mary Bone, is useful, and so is Chapter 5, on identification and dating of military uniforms, by David J Barnes. Chapter 9, 'A Case Study', by Howell Green, I found particularly interesting reading.

The National Museum of Photographs at Bradford has a display of the various old kinds of photographs and if you take yours along, you will be able to compare them with the display and thus work out how old they are, probably to within a few years.

GRAVESTONES

To people who are not tracing their families gravestones and other memorial inscriptions may seem a morbid subject. In fact they can become a fascination, and there is nowhere pleasanter and more of a break from the work-a-day world on a summer's evening than a country churchyard with trees and birdsong.

In about 1837 Cemetery Companies began to be set up, and the large cemeteries we know today were created. There were several reasons for this. With the growth of population the ancient churchyards were faced with a crisis; there was just not enough space, and also, though the residents of a parish had the right to be buried in the parish churchyard, many of the Nonconformist sects did not wish to be buried in the consecrated ground of the churchyard.

Congregationalists and other sects were active in the campaigns for secular burial places. You will occasionally find references to people buried in unconsecrated ground, and you may find that part of a large cemetery is used for the burial of members of the Church of England and other parts for Nonconformists. There may also be a section for the Jews. These very large cemeteries are often now under threat of clearance and in clearing them we lose an enormous amount of history. Sometimes a record is kept of the names on the stones but the names alone are not what is valuable. It is the extra information – the relationships, the snippets like 'forty years an organist' or 'formerly of Weston-super-Mare' or 'died by falling under a bus' (in the days of horse-buses) – which is interesting, and the ages at death, which then give you the approximate date of birth. A gravestone may well prove or disprove something about your family history and that proof disappear for ever if the cemetery is cleared because it is overgrown and difficult to maintain. It is also interesting to read the pious texts and wonder why they were chosen, to note the shape and the embellishments of carving.

Most Family History Societies throughout the British Isles are, as one of their voluntary activities, engaged in transcribing in full the words on all the memorial inscriptions in their areas, a long task and a laborious and time-consuming one, though very interesting. It is always worth asking whether your ancestor's inscription has been recorded – and just hope it has, before the bulldozers get at it. The Family History Society nearest to where the cemetery or churchyard is should be able to tell you. (More of the Societies later.)

The Cemetery Companies kept careful records of the burials and by enquiry you may be able to find where these are and to discover the information in them. It is impossible to give much of a guideline as each case is different. If there is an index to the record books, which there often is, it is easy to find the record of the burial of an ancestor provided you have some idea when they died. The actual entry may then tell you the age, address, cause of death, the officiating clergyman, and probably other details about the burial. What it will not tell you is the inscription on the gravestone, and it is the gravestones which are so often in danger of destruction.

Naturally burials went on in the churchyards, even though the Cemetery Companies were set up. Country churchyards are still in use today. There is often no grave plan or other way of finding a grave except by going and looking, hoping it is not too overgrown. Town churchyards are different, because after the cholera epidemics they were recognised to be a danger to public health and most were closed. I met one person who very quickly traced their family for several generations as they had lived in the same village for a long time and the gravestones were very informative.

FINDING THE HARD FACTS

When you have been asking the family and searching out what is already known for some time, you will feel that you have come to a full stop. You should have some facts and a lot of unsubstantiated stories, some actual documentary evidence, perhaps some photographs with or without names to them. How are you to tie it all together and find out more?

In each of our ancestors' lives there are three main events – if you like, their vital statistics – birth, marriage and death. If you are going to progress with your work on the family you need to find out and verify the facts about these three main events, and that will build up a sound framework for all your other discoveries.

There are many kinds of records which you can consult and these fall into two types – primary and secondary sources.

Not everyone uses the same definition of primary and secondary sources. Strictly speaking, a primary source is the original and usually official record of the event. Historians regard everything handwritten at the time as a primary source, and things printed at the time like newspapers can at times also be included.

Secondary sources include books written about past events, and other people's transcriptions of written records (with some exceptions).

Different sources give you different things. Let us take the example of a wedding. If someone married in England and Wales between 1837 and today, there should exist a marriage certificate for them – an official record of the event, which tells you certain things. There might or might not be a piece about the wedding in the local paper. That would be a subjective account of the accompanying circumstances and celebrations, and probably tells you much more, such as what the bride and bridesmaids wore and even sometimes a list of the presents. But the only thing you should be able to find without fail is the marriage certificate.

Do not forget when searching for these hard facts, to note the source and date of all information found, and to make a note of all *negative* information – that is, note that in such and such a record you found nothing. Strange though it may seem, this negative information can at times be as useful as positive information.

Your journey back to 1939

The principal sources you can use for this part of the journey are:

Oral history and family traditions
Civil registration records
Wills
Electoral registers
Newspapers
Records of the 1939–1945 war
Directories and telephone directories
Family letters, diaries, postcards, other writings
Photographs
Gravestones

Your journey back to 1914

Principal sources are:

Oral history and family traditions
Civil registration records
Wills

Electoral registers
Newspapers
Records of the 1914–1918 war
Family letters etc.
Photographs
Gravestones
Directories

Your journey back to 1881

Oral history and family traditions
Civil registration records
Wills
Records of the Boer War
Postcards
Photographs
Gravestones
Directories

Your journey back to 1865

Civil registration records (ages at death after 1866)
Wills
Census for 1881, 1871
Gravestones
International Genealogical Index (I.G.I.)
Directories

Your journey back to 1837

Civil registration records
Wills
Census for 1861, 1851, 1841
I.G.I.
Directories

From 1881 back to 1837, the three-pronged attack –
civil registration, wills, and census, using each in
combination with the others – will discover the history
of most families in that period. A great help is the I.G.I.
from about 1875.

In any of these periods of time there may be other sources which are useful to you – memorabilia, family papers, or some of the secondary sources mentioned, which help on the way – and some of the sources may overlap into a period where they are not mentioned in these lists.

It helps to think of the various periods through which your ancestors lived; you will understand better the meaning of what you find.

Electoral Registers

This is one of the few sources that are far more useful for recent times than for earlier ones. Registers of Electors should be found in the local reference library for the area where your family lived. In the case of a large town they can run to many volumes, so you need to have a reasonably accurate idea of where people were. For a smaller town, such as York, there is often only one volume and though it may be confusing, split into electoral wards and so on, it does not take very long to go through a single volume, particularly if it is in alphabetical order within each street, as many of them are. These records can be invaluable for the period back to the 1914–18 war. The voters in a household are named and, if you can find the household in successive registers, when one of the voters in that household is no longer shown it is quite likely that, in the case of an older person, they died between the times of the volumes being issued, or, in the case of someone younger, married.

It is often feasible to go through the Register of Electors for your home town and make a note of all families of your name, picking out relatives who you can later connect – if your name is not a common one in the area. It is a useful way of finding out exact addresses, if you have only a vague idea of the place, and sometimes gives an unexpected bonus – for example:

Lodgers. (City of York, 1880)

Dickinson, Thomas Rusholm, (occupies) sitting-room and bedroom furnished, in a dwelling house, 44 Marygate, rent 8s. per week, Landlady Miss Sarah Busby of 44 Marygate.

Voting qualifications have altered over the years, and this affects the usefulness of records of those eligible to vote. A few relevant dates for parliamentary elections are:

1872 Act of Parliament: brought in the Secret Ballot.

1884 Act: brought Household Suffrage to the counties. Many agricultural labourers acquired the vote for the first time, but those in tied houses and with a very low rent still could not vote; nor could any women.

1918 Act: women over thirty could vote in parliamentary elections if they or their husbands owned or occupied property valued at £5 per annum. All men now had the vote regardless of property qualification.

1928 Act: women over twenty-one got the vote.

1948 Act: plural voting for businessmen and University graduates was abolished. Before this they were often entitled to more than one vote each.

The position was not quite the same for local elections, where both men and women have had the vote to a much larger extent.

Civil Registration

One of the things we take for granted in life is the present national system of civil registration. We all know how it works. We look after our birth and marriage certificates and sometimes have to produce them. If a relative dies we may have the task of registering the death. How many of us realise that civil registration began in the year that the seventeen-year-old Queen Victoria came to the throne of England (and the throne also of Scotland, Wales, Ireland and later the Empire)?

All our ancestors back to that momentous year, roughly a century and a half ago, also had birth, marriage and death certificates, and we can obtain copies of them. It is the most enormous thrill to receive a certificate and for the first time to read the extra, new, exact information which the certificate gives.

The method is as follows. Check on what dates you have for the individual you are tracing. Let us suppose that you know your father's date of birth and his father's name, but not his mother's name. There may be no one you can ask. Then, by purchasing a copy of your father's birth certificate, you discover his mother's former name. This knowledge makes it possible for you to apply for your grandparents' marriage certificate. Once you have that, you know the names of both their fathers. Apply for the birth certificates of your grandparents and you then learn their mothers' names. Then you can apply for your great-grandparents' marriage certificates . . . it ought to be as simple as that.

Let us start again at the beginning, looking at the whole system of civil registration, and see how we can learn as much as possible from it with the least effort and expense to ourselves.

Many national records are released for study when they are a hundred years old and it is hoped that soon civil registration details will be so treated; but at present in England and Wales it is not the case.

In theory, the way of using civil registration to trace your family is simple and easy but in practice it may well be quite difficult. We can look at it in the five regions:

1) England and Wales
2) Scotland
3) Ireland
4) Isle of Man
5) Channel Islands

FEES AND EVEN ADDRESSES CAN CHANGE VERY QUICKLY
SO IF YOU ARE MAKING A LONG JOURNEY TO A RECORD
OFFICE CHECK FIRST THAT CONDITIONS ARE STILL THE
SAME.

1) England and Wales

When civil registration was first begun in March 1837
(the first Index books are dated 1 July 1837, and the
entries in them should cover what we now call the
June quarter), existing divisions of the country were
used, based on Poor Law Unions of parishes, and on
other parishes or places governed under the Poor Laws
by Boards of Guardians. A reorganisation was carried
out in 1851 and another in 1947. Often, if our ancestors
came from another part of the country, the names of
the areas will not seem familiar to us. Every quarter of
the year – that is, every three months – the local
registrars list all the births, marriages and deaths
they have registered in that three months and send the
list to the Registrar General. At the office of the
Registrar General one large consolidated index is
made, so that it is easy to find the copy of the original
certificate, no matter which part of the country it has
come from.

Records are still kept locally in the office of the area
registrar of births, marriages and deaths and it is
possible to buy a certificate from a local registrar.
Often, however, it is better to use the Registrar General's consolidated indexes in St Catherine's House,
which run from 1 July 1837 to within a year of the
present day.

Why?

Because although you may have an expensive journey to London, once there you are allowed to search through the indexes for as long as you like, *free*. A lot may be gained from such a search in addition to whatever certificates you decide to purchase. If you wished to search the indexes at a local registrar's office, you would have to make special arrangements with the local registrar, who might find it inconvenient to accomodate you, and you would pay quite a heavy charge per half day. It is more than likely that you would not find the entry you were seeking and would then have to visit London anyway. When the right information is at last located you may find that your ancestor was born at his granny's house, married when he was in the Army and stationed in Bombay, and died on holiday at the seaside . . . none of which was at all what you expected. Use the national index and you will save yourself a lot of time.

So. Armed with the information you have amassed, you plan a visit to London. The correct postal address is:

The Registrar General
St Catherine's House
10 Kingsway
London WC2B 6JP
(tel. (01) 242 0262)

Although the Aldwych is the nearest Tube station, it is not always open, so it is best to go to Holborn. Walk down Kingsway for about ten minutes to the corner where it meets the semi-circular Aldwych; St Catherine's House is on this corner.

You may look at the indexes between the hours of 8.30 a.m. and 4.30 p.m. Monday to Friday; they are closed all day on public holidays.

Leaflets CAS 63, CAS 1, and CAS 1a, available from St Catherine's, give general information.

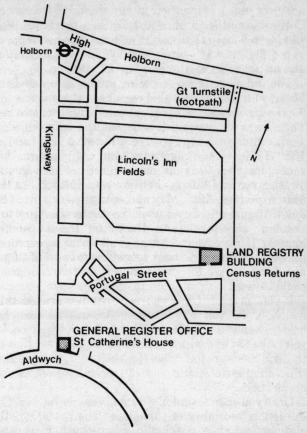

St Catherine's is a very busy place. It is possible that first thing in the morning or last thing in the afternoon on a foggy January day it might be fairly quiet, but usually it is like the first day of the sales. You need to be well prepared, to have worked out all you can in advance, to know just what you are going to look for and to have something ready in which to write the information, if you are to make the most of your visit –

and everyone tracing their family should try to visit St Catherine's at least once just for the experience. You will learn a lot in that visit. You must also be prepared in a different way – dress simply, do not carry much and do not take anything valuable with you.

The indexes are large books, arranged on shelves. Make your way to the shelves where the indexes are for the right event, and right years, and start looking. The sets of shelves are labelled on the ends with the years and the type of record, such as, BIRTHS 1850–1890. As the registrars send their information each quarter of the year, the indexes are arranged in quarter years: January, February and March are the March quarter; April, May and June the June quarter; July, August and September the September quarter; October, November and December the December quarter. If there were not many entries for one particular quarter, then one book might contain all of them, but if there were too many then more than one book could be used.

If you have provided yourself with a way of noting which books you have looked at, such as the grid below, then you will know afterwards just which books you looked at and which you didn't. You will see that in the grid there are four boxes for each year, to represent the four quarters, and you can tick them off as you check them.

Once you open an index volume, what do you see? On the left is a column of surnames. The list is strictly alphabetical, like a telephone directory. First, the surnames are listed alphabetically and then within that surname the Christian names are alphabetical. In the 'births', last of all come those children who are registered before their parents have decided on a name, so that they are registered only as male or female.

It follows that if there are two books for one quarter, one will cover the first half of the alphabet and the

RESEARCH CHART – ST CATHERINE'S HOUSE

Ancestor's Name _____ FANNY BAKER _____

Birth/Marriage/Death ___ BIRTH _____

Year	Quarterly volumes				Found District	Vol. no.	Page no.
	Mar	Jun	Sep	Dec			
1841	✓	✓	✓	✓			
1842	✓	✓			ROMFORD	VII	134

Example

other the second, and the letters covered by each book will be given on the spine.

When you have found the name you are looking for, look at the other columns.

These have changed a little over the years. Here are some examples of the way the columns have been laid out:

BIRTHS, 1837 *Name*	*Superintendent Registrar's District*		*Vol.* *Page*
Smith, Ellen	Salford		xx 407
BIRTHS, 1966 *Name of child*	*Mother's maiden name*	*Reference District*	*Vol.* *Page*
Smith, Ellen	Jones	Durham W	1A 1008
MARRIAGES, 1837 *Surname of person married*	*Name of the same*	*District*	*Vol.* *Page*
Smith	Ellen	Leeds	xxiii 418
MARRIAGES, 1983 *Names of persons*	*Married*	*Reference District*	*Vol.* *Page*
Smith, Ellen	Jones	Wigan	39 2453
DEATHS, 1837 *Name*	*Superintendent Registrar's District*		*Vol.* *Page*
Smith, Ellen	St George's, Hanover Square, Stepney		I 6
DEATHS, 1956 *Name*	*Age*	*District*	*Vol.* *Page*
Smith, Ellen	83	Kettering	36 414

If you are sure the certificate reference you have found will be for the one you want, copy the details in your notebook and go to fill in an application form and pay for the certificate.

The charge at the time of writing is £5 for a full certificate. (For family history purposes the short certificates are no use at all.) This is if you apply for the certificate when you are there. If you write to ask for it, even if you can supply the exact details, the cost is £10.

If you order a certificate and can call back to collect it, you may be able to have it in a couple of days. If it is sent to you by post it will take much longer.

Information is not supplied by the Registrar General except in the form of certificates; but actually it is surprising how much information may be gleaned from the indexes alone, once you get used to them. For instance, you might notice that the people of your surname mostly seem to come from one area; or you may notice the registrations of your grandfather's brothers and sisters, and be able to note down the quarter when they appear without actually buying certificates; or you may be looking for a particular marriage, and in passing note down other marriages in the same area for people of the same surname, and discover later that these are relatives.

If you are looking for a marriage you should have worked out in advance in which year it was most likely to have taken place, calculating by the date of birth of the eldest child. It is wise to begin looking actually at the quarter in which the birth took place, and then work backwards in time. The eldest child of the marriage might have been born before the ceremony or very soon after. On the other hand there may well have been an earlier child who died in infancy and whom no one in the family now knows about. It is a fairly safe rule of thumb that you should find the marriage in the five years before the birth of the eldest child. If not, try looking through the year or two later.

Sometimes people search through twenty years before finding the marriage they are seeking, but you should not be so unlucky.

Starting with the March quarter for 1866, the age at death is given in the indexes of death registrations, though in family history one learns to take all ages at death as slightly dubious until they are confirmed by other data. It is amazingly easy to forget exactly how old someone was, if they belonged to the generation before your own. From the June quarter for 1969 the date of birth is also given.

Starting with the September quarter for 1911, the maiden name of the mother is included in the indexes of birth registrations, which helps you to identify all the children of a certain marriage in the subsequent years.

Starting with the March quarter for 1912, in marriage registrations the surname of the second party to the marriage will also be shown so that you should know at once if you have the right entry.

With marriages, you should always begin by looking for the most unusual name as it is the quickest to find. People with unusual names have a flying head start in family history. If your grandfather was William Clark and your grandmother was Lavinia Hawthornthwaite, then begin looking for Hawthornthwaite; there will not be as many of them as there are of the Clarks. When you find one of the names you are looking for, after 1912 the other person's name should also be there. Before 1912 you should cross check. Note which quarter of which year it is and the exact details of the entry. Look in the same quarter of the same year for the other partner's name. If it is there and if it gives *exactly* the same reference details, then the two names appear on the same certificate and you have found the one you seek.

If you had a lot of information to begin with you could now go on to look for the next certificate you need. It helps if you go with several queries – perhaps on different branches of the family – so that if one search is fruitless you can make another. But in practice this is not always possible. You might need the new information from one certificate to identify the next sufficiently. It works in a stepping-stone fashion. A birth certificate gives you the name and former name of the child's mother. You need this information before you can be sure of obtaining the correct marriage certificate. The marriage certificate will give you the name of the fathers of both bride and groom and then you will be able to look for their birth certificates.

If the father's name is *not* given on a birth certificate it normally means that the person was illegitimate. If the father's name is not given on a marriage certificate it can also mean that the person marrying was illegitimate, though in the case of a marriage it might perhaps mean that a young couple were trying to conceal the marriage. Our ancestors were just as likely to tell little white lies as we are ourselves and though you can often discover the fibs and go on tracing the family, they can throw you off the scent for a while.

If your research is held up because you cannot visit London in person, you can write to the Registrar General at St Catherine's and order a certificate by post. They will search through five years of indexes for you. For example, if you think an event took place in 1920 and give that date, they will also search through 1918, 1919, 1921 and 1922. This can be very useful but it does add to your costs as you will be charged an extra £5 for the search even if the certificate is found straight away – even if you gave them the exact information they needed to find it. That is why certificates are £10 by post but only £5 if you request them on the spot, giving all the correct information.

Sometimes, no matter how careful you are, you find that you have bought the wrong certificate. Don't worry too much. All that has happened is that you have wasted some money – but one buys experience, and you will be more careful still next time.

It is possible to give 'checking points' if you are not sure whether or not you have chosen the right entry from the indexes, or when applying by post, which the Registrar General's staff can check and thus select the right certificate. This can be a great help and stop you buying the wrong one in error. There is a different form if you wish them to do this and slightly different payment arrangements. Form CAS 62 from St Catherine's explains exactly how this method works.

It follows that if you want several certificates, it pays you to visit St Catherine's in person. You should be able to save the cost of your transport at least, and you can probably find additional information while you are there. Keep that accurate record of which index volumes you have looked at.

The volumes are large and heavy and to look over a long span of years is tiring. But many people with unusual names do go right through the indexes making a note of every entry for their name (without of course actually ordering the certificates). Before you go to such lengths it would be wise to find out if anyone else has already undertaken this massive task. We will deal later with how to find other people searching for the same name.

Microfilm of the indexes
There is another way to look at the indexes. The Mormon Church has microfilmed them and these microfilms are widely available at Mormon branch libraries throughout the country. The contribution made by the Mormon Church will be dealt with more fully under the later section dealing with the International Genealogical Index (I.G.I.).

You can also buy a certificate from the registrar in the place where the event took place. This is not only cheaper but also quicker. When I lost my birth certificate, for instance, I did not need to go to St Catherine's. I simply wrote to the registrar's office in the city where I was born, quoting my date of birth and the address of my birthplace. Local registrars only charge £5 even if they sell you a certificate through the post, but on the other hand you cannot expect them to spend ages looking through records for you. They do not have the advantage of a consolidated index like the one held by the Registrar General. If you quote them an index reference from St Catherine's it does not help them at all. Marriages may be entered under several different churches as well as in a separate list for the Register Office itself.

If you know the exact date and place of an event it is sensible to write to the local registrar instead of the Registrar General. You will save money. But it is very often more economical in time and everything else to use that marvellous consolidated index. You can waste a lot of time, other people's as well as your own, looking for an event in the wrong place.

One lady, for instance, told her children which chapel she was married in, but in fact she was married in the Register Office, and this was in 1883, earlier than one would have expected such a form of marriage to be popular. In another case, a Yorkshire farmer was married in St George's, Hanover Square, London, as he was a Guardsman at the time. His descendants could never have guessed that he had been married there.

People often wish to look in church records for baptisms, marriages and burials for this recent period, but in practice it is time wasting unless you have concrete evidence of where the event took place. That is why this book hardly deals at all with church registers. If you *do* have concrete evidence that an event took place after 1837 in a specific church or chapel, then you can approach the local church authorities and ask if the registers are still in the church (or chapel), but when you reach an earlier period of time you will rely heavily on Church records. It seems more sensible where there is a simpler method, to use it.

Other records in St Catherine's House
The Registrar General holds other records which can most appropriately be mentioned here. The Overseas Section, for instance, has such things as an *Index to Regimental Registers, 1761–1924, Marine Births* of various dates, *Consular Births* (births recorded by the British consuls abroad; they also recorded deaths and marriages), an *Index to Naval War Deaths, 3 September 1939 to 10 June 1948*, and so on. These are the titles of some of the volumes on the shelves of this section. If you have reason to think that your family events may have taken place abroad this would be where to look. The St Catherine's leaflet dealing with these records is CAS 2.

Scotland

Lucky indeed are those with Scottish ancestry! At the General Register Office (which is at New Register House) in Edinburgh, are the three main sources of hard facts for family history in Scotland for the last two hundred and fifty years: the civil registration records, the census returns, and the parish registers of before 1855. The General Register Office is near the end of Princes Street behind the Scottish Record Office, and only a few minutes' walk from the railway station. If you possibly can, visit Edinburgh to carry out your own research, and try to do so when the office is less busy – say, between September and May. During the summer months many visitors, including those from overseas, will be tracing their ancestors! Here is the full postal address:

The General Register Office for Scotland
New Register House
Princes Street
Edinburgh EH1 3YT
(tel. (031) 556-3952)

Opening hours are Monday to Thursday 9.30–4.30,
Friday 9.30–4.00.

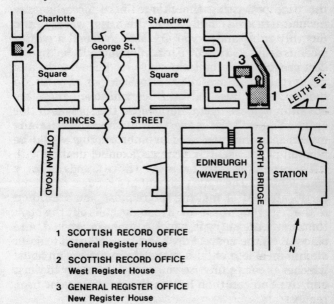

1 SCOTTISH RECORD OFFICE
  General Register House

2 SCOTTISH RECORD OFFICE
  West Register House

3 GENERAL REGISTER OFFICE
  New Register House

There are four main differences between Scottish civil
registration and that of England and Wales.

Firstly, in Scotland the system did not commence
until 1 January 1855.

Secondly, although the system began later, this
disadvantage is counterbalanced by the fact that
Scottish certificates give much more information –

41

particularly about that first year, when so much information was asked for that it was found to be impractical, after which less was asked for. The Scottish system is an extraordinarily bountiful source when compared with civil registration in the rest of the British Isles.

Thirdly, you must pay if you make a personal visit and wish to see the indexes, for a day or half a day. At the time of writing the charge is £8 for a one-day inclusive search, but there are also weekly and monthly rates and if you are able to spend a winter week tracing your Scottish family you will be able to do a great deal in the time.

Fourthly, you are allowed to look not only at the indexes, but also at the certificates, and this advantage more than outweighs the payment for entry. You will not have to wait for weeks for the information that you need in order to progress to the next bit of your search; you can go on at once.

The procedure is that when you have found the entry you require in the index, you put in a request to see the certificates. After making the request, you are taken to the registers where an attendant pulls out the book containing the entry in which you are interested, and places it on the nearest desk. You are allowed to see a maximum of four entries *or* spend a quarter of an hour, whichever comes first, so you need to be ready to work quickly. You can then look in the index for your next request.

It is also possible to write for information by post.

Ireland

If you have Irish ancestors, it would help to know from the family approximately when they left Ireland (assuming that they did). Obviously if they settled in England they will appear in the English records after that date. If they came over at the time of the great famine in 1846 or 1847 then you will be able to use the records mentioned for England during most of the period covered by this book.

If possible, find out the religion of the family and the parish from which they came, and an approximate date. Irish families are more difficult to trace in any case, because of the amount of records which have been destroyed, but a lot can still be done.

Civil registration began in Ireland on 1 January 1864, but Protestant marriages had to be registered earlier, from 1845. The records for the whole of Ireland up to 1921 are at the following address:

The Registrar General
Joyce House
8–11 Lombard Street East
Dublin 2
Republic of Ireland
(tel. (0001) 711000)

You could do with a map to find it if you are visiting Dublin. Lombard Street East is off Pearse Street. The office you want is on the first floor, at the time of writing. A fee is payable for looking at the indexes, at present £1 for five years in one type of index, i.e. either the birth, or marriage or death index. You can also pay a higher fee (£11.00) for an unlimited search in any category. If you find the entry you require in the index you may request a photocopy of the certificate for a fee of £1.50 and will receive it in a few minutes. The indexes are like those at St Catherine's House and the certificates give the same information as those for England and Wales. It is possible to request a certificate by post but it may well be very slow in coming.

The records for the years after 1921 for the Irish Repubic are still in Dublin, but those for Northern Ireland are at this address:

The Registrar General
Oxford House
49–55 Chichester Street
Belfast BT1 4HL
Northern Ireland
(tel. (0232) 235211)

When writing with enquiries, enclose a large stamped
addressed envelope when writing to Belfast, and a large
self-addressed envelope with an international reply
coupon, which you can buy at a post office, when writing
to Dublin.

Isle of Man

In the Isle of Man, registration of births and of deaths
began in 1878 and registration of marriages in 1884.
Write for an application form to:

The Chief Registrar
General Registry
Finch Road
Douglas
Isle of Man

You can then apply for a full birth, marriage or death
certificate at a cost of £2.25 each. Search fees, if you
cannot give the exact information, are 75p a year for the
first year and 30p for each additional year. There is also
the adopted children register which dates back to 1928.

As the civil registration system began so late in the
Isle of Man, church records have to be used for the period
back to 1837, and fortunately the Chief Registrar can
supply certificates from some church records also, i.e.,
baptisms (Church of England only); marriages (Church
of England and Dissenter marriages, 1849–1883, and
Church of England only, prior to that); burials (Church
of England only).

Channel Islands

The Channel Islands fall into two different jurisdictions: Alderney, Sark and Herm come under Guernsey; Jersey is separate.

Guernsey

Births, deaths and marriages have been registered under a civil registration system in Guernsey since 1840. If you visit the island, it is possible to carry out a search yourself for a fee of £1. If you write, the fee for a search is £1 and a certificate is £1.50. You need to supply as much information as possible and it is best to write first, to:

> The Registrar General of Births, Marriages and
> Deaths
> Greffe
> Royal Court House
> St Peter Port
> Guernsey
> Channel Islands

Jersey

Births, marriages and deaths have been registered under a civil registration system in Jersey since August, 1842. Although in theory the records are publicly available, they are so complex to use that research is done by the staff on behalf of enquirers. The search fee is £8 per hour, but as the staff are very experienced they can search much more quickly than a member of the public could. There is a charge of £4 for each extract from the records. The address to write to is:

> The Superintendent Registrar
> States Office
> Royal Square
> St Helier
> Jersey
> Channel Islands

BACK TO THE
FAMILY TREE

Look at the family tree you have drawn so far. Have you found the three vital statistics for the lives of those people you have included in it? You may not need them for everyone. It is probably enough to have rough ideas of the dates of various uncles and aunts, and people are often happy to enter approximate dates of death. As far as buying certificates goes, you need only buy key ones, thus keeping your expenditure down, but you should try not to skip the really essential ones, or dreadful errors will creep in.

You can ask your relatives for more exact details the next time you meet. For the most important people in your family tree you must try to have that firm framework: for your parents, their parents, and the line which you are specifically following back.

Basic information should be included on your tree:

> JOHN GREEN
> born 29 December 1902
> at Tynmouth
> Engineer of Sheffield
> died 30th March 1959
> at Croydon

This can be simplified to:

> JOHN GREEN
> b. 29 Dec. 1902
> Engineer
> d. 30 Mar. 1959

Until recent times, women tended not to state their jobs on their marriage certificates, so the line taken up by naming a man's work can be free to give the date of the marriage:

JOHN GREEN   =   MARY BROWN
b. 29 Dec.1902   b. 29 Sept. 1904
Engineer   m.16 Apr. 1928
d. 30 Mar. 1959   d. 23 Dec. 1979

It is quite likely, given a little luck, that you will be able to identify the births of children of a marriage in the indexes with reasonable certainty, so that without buying the certificates for everyone in a big family you can gain a good idea of their dates of birth.

When you obtain any certificate examine it carefully. It will yield a lot of information.

Birth Certificates

The most important piece of information you want is the maiden (or former) name of the child's mother, so that you can go on to locate the marriage certificate. Apart from this, the certificate tells you in which district and sub-district the birth took place; probably the actual address where the baby was born; who notified the birth; the names of both parents; the former name of the mother; the occupation of the father. If the father is not named it is usually a case of illegitimacy and often this can be a stone wall on that particular line. But there are always other lines you can follow, and sometimes the father is named even if the couple were not married; or the child is given his father's surname as a Christian name, which may enable you to identify him.

Note that the mother's 'former' name may be, if she marries more than once, either her maiden name or her previous married name.

You are also given the name, description and address of the informant. It is interesting in early entries to notice how often the mother herself went to register the birth only a day or two after the child was born.

Marriage Certificates

All the information – and there is a mass of it – should be noted. Religious denominations are important, and who the witnesses were. Witnesses were often relatives and can be identified, or are friends who may reappear later in the family story.

A marriage certificate will tell you when and where the marriage took place and the names, ages, addresses, occupations and marital status of bride and groom, together with the names and occupations of their fathers and the names of the witnesses.

Death Certificates

Finding the right entry in the indexes may well tell you all you need to know. As mentioned before, after 1866 the age at death is given. Do not forget that this may be a guess on the part of the person who registered the death. Sometimes it does seem worth while buying a copy of the death certificate. It may prove or disprove some family story – such as that the person died of sunstroke due to harvesting in the fields. Or it may help to locate where the family were living at the time, which could enable you to find them in a census. If information is so scarce about a family that any scrap is of help, the name of the informant who told the registrar of the death may be useful – often a wife, husband, son or daughter. If the person lived most of his or her life before the start of civil registration it may be reassuring to have at least one certificate with positive and definite information to assist the next stage of the journey back in time.

It has perhaps become obvious to you already, while

reading about civil registration, how very helpful it is when tracing family history to have an unusual surname. An unusual Christian name, from the days when children were named after their grandparents or other members of the family, can also be a great help. Faced with a page full of entries for (say) Clarke or Wilson, you may well wish that your name had been Tolpuddle or Scatterbrain. But a more usual name need not make you despair – it only makes your task harder. Even a very uncommon name may occur frequently in one particular locality. People who make quick progress at first, because they are the only family of Splashes in Yorkshire, may have difficulty when they reach earlier times and discover that Splash was the most common name in the village of Wharram Simon, from where the various Splash families spread out.

SURNAMES

Before the fourteenth century there were very few surnames and they were rather changeable, but during that century they became more widespread and soon everyone found it useful to have one. They have never had the immutability of Christian names; once a name has been given in baptism it is virtually unchangeable, but a surname you may legally change at will, if you wish, by telling everyone that in future you wish to be known by a different one. Changes by deed poll give a feeling of extra legality but are not essential.

Surnames arose in four ways. They came from:

1. A place
2. An occupation
3. A personal characteristic
4. Parentage

If you imagine a medieval village with four men called John and subsequent confusion, you can see how they could be called

John from Haxby (John de Haxby)
John the Butcher
John Redhead
John Nell's son.

1. Many villages would have a butcher, a baker, a smith, and so on, therefore names from occupations tend to be more widespread. The families may originally have had no connection at all with each other and are often the most difficult to trace because numerous. As you move back in time the position

sometimes becomes easier because however many Smith families arose, yours might be the only one in your particular area.

2. Place names can also be borne by many quite unrelated families, who only have in common that they left that place six centuries before. Some families took the name of a place because they happened to own it, which may give you a hint of possible former grandeur! As well as the names of towns and villages, families may have names from a smaller landscape feature – Wood, or Green, or Hill, or Rowbottom (a bottom being a valley) or Attlee (at the clearing). *The Oxford Dictionary of English Place-names* by Eilert Ekwall will give you a good idea of the meaning of names which are derived from proper names of places.

3. Names deriving from personal characteristics are on the whole less widespread as they were more individual. Whitehead, Redhead and so on could arise separately in many different places, but Clothears or Spindleshanks may well have been the name originally of only one family.

4. Names from parentage can arise from either the father or the mother – Robson, Nelson. In many countries these changed with each generation and this is still the custom in Scandinavia. In Wales the custom went on until fairly recent times, this accounting for the many families called Pritchard (*Ap Richard*, son of Richard) and so on. In this group we could put the allegiance names of Scotland, which show not necessarily relationship but clan loyalty.

Books on names published in the past are full of inaccuracies but more recently better work has been done on surnames. The *English Surnames* series, general editor R A McKinley, is a great advance on former books. The first volume contains Dr Redmonds' work on the surnames of the West Riding of Yorkshire. Names of any type can have been singular in origin – given to one man only and now only used by the descendants of that man. Dr Redmonds has shown pretty conclusively that this is the case for some Yorkshire names. The second volume covers early Norfolk and Suffolk surnames; the third volume, Oxfordshire. This series should eventually cover the whole of England.

Names can have a regional character. Many of us notice when we are in another part of the country that the local names are strange to us. Cornish names, Suffolk names, Manx names – many areas have this homogeneity. If the members of your family come from one area, you soon learn to recognise the names of that area.

MORE HARD FACTS

Wills since 1858 in England and Wales

Just as the civil registration records are a primary source of information, so are the wills for which probate has been obtained, and the letters of administration. Wills proved before 1858 are a different matter, and will not be dealt with in this book, but in January of that year they began to be proved legally valid by the same nationwide system of probate registries and sub-registries that we use today.

Tracing back to 1837, we should find that the records of this nationally organised system, which are very easy to use and deal with everyone alive after 1858, are enough for our purposes. Every will which has been left in England and Wales since January, 1858, and legally proved, is entered in the index which you may see free of charge at the Principal Probate Registry, Somerset House, Strand, London. See map.

You may think that your ancestors were not the kind of people to leave wills. However, a casual glance at the index shows a labourer whose worldly goods amounted to £2 in value and whose will was proved, so there is a good chance that any one of us may find wills for our family, even if they lived in humble circumstances. Many people left them who were not rich – in fact it is wise for all of us to leave a will.

The index for wills may also be seen at certain other probate offices throughout the country, so before you make the journey to Somerset House it is worth enquiring at your nearest office to see whether they have a set. If they have, it will be exactly the same as the one

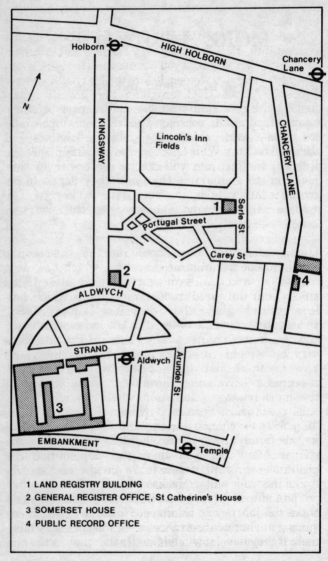

1 LAND REGISTRY BUILDING
2 GENERAL REGISTER OFFICE, St Catherine's House
3 SOMERSET HOUSE
4 PUBLIC RECORD OFFICE

in Somerset House, and will cover the *whole* of England and Wales since 1858.

Having established the date when an ancestor died, it is as well to check whether they made a will. You can save up the details, until you have several to check on. In the case of married women, before the Married Women's Property Act of 1892, anything they owned before marriage automatically became the property of their husbands after the ceremony, so they did not usually leave wills. Widows and single women, however, did leave wills. These can be most useful, particularly the wills of maiden aunts who liked to remember all their nephews and nieces, and may give you the details of the complete family.

If married women owned property before 1892 it had usually been settled on them legally in such a way that their husbands could not spend it, and often was to go on to their children automatically after their deaths, in which case no will was necessary.

If you go to look at the index to wills at a local probate office, you will need to fit in with the individual arrangements of the office. There may be certain days, for instance, when they will be too busy to want an extra person on the premises, dinner-time may be inconvenient for them – in short, contact them and, if they do have a copy of the index, ask how and when it will be convenient for you to go to use it for the purpose of tracing your ancestors.

In the case of Somerset House, you can go along Monday to Friday between the hours of 10 a.m. and 4.30 p.m. You may be asked the purpose of your visit by the official on the door. You should then be admitted to a pleasant room with the indexes in low bookshelves round the walls and in blocks in the centre.

The index is printed for each year; for earlier years there will only be one volume per year. For more recent years it might have been necessary to split the index into more than one volume, alphabetically.

Letters of administration are issued when there is no will and it is necessary to have authority to administer the goods of the dead person. Make sure that you examine those, too. They may be mixed in with the entries for wills, in which case you cannot miss seeing them, but in earlier years they were often entered at the back or front of the volume, and need checking separately.

Modern entries in the index are rather shorter than earlier ones but they are always very informative – far more informative than the indexes for civil registration. Here is an example:

> Johnson Staniforth Hill. Personal estate £295 3s 2d. 7 September, 1889. The will of Johnson Staniforth Hill formerly of Newland but late of Epworth both in the county of Lincoln Farmer who died 8 June, 1888, at Epworth was proved at Lincoln by Ann Hill of Epworth Widow the Relict the sole Executrix.

The system with wills is that the original is taken to the probate office by the dead person's family, or by their solicitor. When it is proved legally valid, or when letters of administration are granted, the executors who are to carry out the terms of the will are given a copy, the original is retained in the probate office, and a second copy is sent to Somerset House. It follows that if you are looking at the will index at Somerset House, they will also have a copy there, which you will be able to see on request. You can then take notes from it, or ask for a photocopy. The charge for a photocopy is at the time of writing 25p per sheet plus £1 handling charge. (It is worth knowing that if you make notes from a will or copy out part of it, this is called an 'abstract'.)

You may also buy a photocopy from the Principal Probate Registry by post, if you have looked at the index elsewhere, or if you have made a note of a will from the index and decide at some later date that you would like a copy. When writing, give the exact details as set out in the index and be careful to include the name of the probate registry where the will was proved. You will be sent an invoice telling you how much it will cost and on their receipt of your payment you will be sent the copy.

The position is more complicated at local probate offices; due to lack of space the wills may have been sent elsewhere for storage, or they may not have copying facilities. Wills are legal documents and special conditions have to be observed in the matter of copying them.

It may surprise you that it is so easy to see a will proved after 1858, but is an essential safeguard against fraud that wills should be public documents.

It might be that, although you know one of your ancestors was in a good way of business, you can find no will, not even an administration. This could be for a number of reasons. The property might have been disposed of before a person's death. Buildings and land were rented much more commonly than they are today, so that apart from cash in hand and investments there may have been little to dispose of, particularly if the tenancy was taken over by a member of the family and the business or farm carried on. Many widows carried on their husbands' businesses. If they took over rented property this did not need to be dealt with by will. Also, if money was entailed in a family or left in trust, this was already tied up legally and no further arrangements were needed. Also, a person might have had an income in the form of an annuity, which would die with them.

Wills in Scotland

Wills in Scotland are usually referred to as 'testaments'. Those dating from 1876 are easy to use;

there is an annual list and the records are housed and indexed in the Scottish Record Office at Register House, Princes Street, Edinburgh. There are so many different types of records in their care that they are now split and some of them are in West Register House in Charlotte Street. For the beginner in family history, the records at West Register House are not likely to be very useful. (There is a large collection of maps and plans there.) Access to the Scottish Records Office is free; you go to the Historical Search Room and apply for a reader's ticket.

From 1823 to 1876, wills were proved by sheriff's courts, and although most of them are in the Scottish Record Office, not all of them are there. This may present difficulties, but you will be able to discover where they are, if they are not at the Record Office.

Wills in Ireland

For wills dating from 1858 there is a calendar (which is like an index) to Irish wills and administrations arranged in alphabetical order of surnames in years, similar to the one discussed above under 'England and Wales'. Although very few Irish wills survive, the index itself is very helpful. Write with enquiries to the Public Record Office of either Dublin or Belfast depending on the date the will was proved. All records for the years up to the partition of the country in 1922 will be in Dublin.

The Public Record Office of Northern Ireland is at 66 Balmoral Avenue, Belfast BT9 6NY.

Wills in the Isle of Man

Manx wills dating from 1628 to 1910 are with The Archivist, The Manx Museum and National Trust, Douglas, Isle of Man. Those from 1910 to the present are at the Deeds Registry, General Registry, Finch Road, Douglas, Isle of Man.

Deeds to Property are also at the Deeds Registry and these can be invaluable when tracing a family.

The cost of copies of wills and deeds is at present 10p a sheet plus postage.

Wills in the Channel Islands

In the Channel Islands two wills are made: one for 'realty', which is property of the bricks and mortar kind, and one for 'personalty', which is money, shares, personal effects, etc.

Guernsey
Wills for realty can be examined at the Greffe, Royal Court House, St Peter Port. Wills for personalty are at the Ecclesiastical Court, New Street, St Peter Port. Although these can be seen by the public, the hours when this is possible are very limited. Guernsey also covers Alderney, Herm and Sark.

Jersey
While wills in Jersey are considered to be public records, it is not possible to examine them in person. It would be best to write to enquire in any particular case, to:

Judicial Greffe
10 Hill Street
St Helier
Jersey
Channel Islands

When writing to southern Ireland, the Isle of Man, or the Channel Islands, enclose an international reply coupon instead of stamping your return envelope, as British stamps are not valid there.

FINDING RESEARCH
OTHERS HAVE DONE;
JOINING SOCIETIES

By the time you have found and confirmed your family history back to 1881, it will be worth checking to see if anyone else is also tracing your family, or has already traced them. There is not much point in checking right at the beginning. If one of your close relatives has begun the search you will either already know or will find out when you make your first enquiries in the family. If someone more distantly related is searching, you will in any case have to trace your line of the family back to the point where it meets theirs, so your time will not have been wasted.

There are a number of ways of trying to find out if anyone else is doing the same research, or has done it.

If anyone has actually published a history of your family, this should be shown in the index to the books in the British Library; this index is a large set of books which are in most of the large reference libraries in the country. Looking up your family name in these volumes does not take long, and it is worth doing, though very few people will find anything.

In 1903, G W Marshall published *A Genealogist's Guide*, which was brought more up to date in 1953 by J B Whitmore in his *Genealogical Guide*. Again, these books are often found in reference libraries, and you would be wise to check with them. Since 1953 there has been a great surge in the amount of research being carried out and it is more difficult to keep up with. The Society of Genealogists are compiling a National Register of pedigrees where more than three generations have been traced, and they will check for you for £1 (at present) to see whether your surname is amongst those on the register.

It is also a good idea at this point to consider joining a Family History Society. They have sprung up in all areas of the country and your local library or information bureau should be able to tell you the address of the secretary of the nearest society. Many people join two societies, the one nearest their home so that they can meet other people with the same interest and hear lectures on various topics connected with family history, and one in the area from which their family come. (This can be awkward if your family come from several different places! You may find yourself wondering how many societies to join.) A Family History Society usually publishes lists of its members' interests, so you can find out if anyone else is interested in – say – the Willsons of Boston, or the Clarkes of Camberley. They will also give publicity to your own search so that anyone who can add to your knowledge can get in touch with you. If you have a fairly unusual name, a number of groups have been set up who specialise in this study of certain names; there is a Guild of One-name Studies, who can tell you if there is such a society for your name.

Only two addresses of societies concerned with family history will be given in this book. One is the Society Of Genealogists, who are at 14 Charterhouse Buildings, London EC1M 7BA, and are a nationwide society. They were the first family history society to be founded in this country, and have a permanent headquarters with an unrivalled collection of books and documents on the subject. Even if you are not a member of the society you are allowed to use their library on payment of a fee for a day or half a day. They publish books and leaflets to help you and stock a very good range of other books on the subject of family history and related subjects, which you can buy. If you become a member there is a quarterly magazine. They also publish books and booklets on family history.

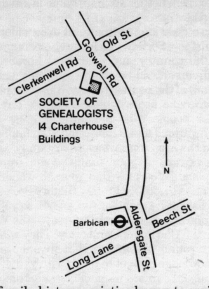

As local family history societies began to spring up all over the country, the need was felt for an organization to help them work together and co-ordinate the study done in each area. The Federation of Family History Societies was formed, and you can write to their Administrator for information. This is, at the time of writing: Mrs P Saul, 31 Seven Star Road, Solihull, West Midlands B91 2BZ. The Federation will be able to tell you the address of your nearest society. They also have a range of publications which are marvellous value and will be very helpful to you as you go on. They have a periodical, *Family History News and Digest*, which keeps everyone up to date with what other societies are doing. They also produce a range of forms on which you can enter your findings and which help to keep your growing records under control.

Other Family History Societies do not have permanent premises as a rule and change their secretaries from time to time, so it is best to make enquiries of the Federation, your local reference library or information bureau, and be supplied with the most up-to-date address for the society you wish to join.

Studying families seems to bring out the best in people! You will find family historians a friendly and helpful crowd.

STILL MORE HARD FACTS.

The Census

The two very important primary sources discussed so far are the civil registration records and the probate records for wills and administrations. Now, having reached back to the year 1881, you can begin to use the third great primary source for the period back to 1837: the census records. Using these three together you should not have too much difficulty in forming a clear picture of the lives of your ancestors during the greater part of the nineteenth century.

It has been known for someone beginning with a good knowledge of where their family lived, and using the census records, to trace them back to the beginning of the nineteenth century in one afternoon, without buying a single birth, marriage or death certificate! (They were a farming family who were still living on the same farm.)

There are many others who have had much more difficulty, but once back to 1881, the three-pronged attack using the primary records should be successful.

You may remember filling in census forms for the most recent census in 1981. A census in Britain was taken for the first time in 1801 and apart from 1941, when none was taken, it has been taken every ten years since that time. Unfortunately, the details of the early censuses were not kept – all we have of them is the totals of males and females living in the various places, and so on. It has happened that in very rare instances one of the enumerator's notebooks has survived from an early census, but this is so rare that for practical purposes you can forget it.

England and Wales

The first census from which details were preserved is that of 1841, so this is the first which is useful to family historians.

Census details are kept secret until a hundred years after the census was taken, so at the time of writing the most recent census which is freely available is that of 1881. Unfortunately for future family historians, the 1931 census was destroyed by fire, and no census was taken in 1941. All the censuses taken later than 1881 remain in the care of the Registrar General, at St Catherine's House. It is possible to obtain a little limited information from the 1891 and 1901 censuses at a considerable fee (£16.75 at time of writing) and with the written consent of the person or of their direct descendant – but it is very limited indeed. The age and place of birth of one named person can be ascertained if you know the address at which the person was living at the time. Only very occasionally, in a state of desperation when all other means of tracing the person have come to brick walls, is it worth your while asking for information from these later censuses; if you do decide to do so, an application form can be obtained from the Registrar-General.

This means that we can use the censuses of 1841, 1851, 1861, 1871, 1881 to help us in our search, and they open for us a direct window into the past. Each census shows us the household of our ancestor family as they were on the night that the census was taken.

These nights were 7 June, 1841, 30 March, 1851, 7 April, 1861, 2 April, 1871 and 4 April, 1881.

The census took place all over the country on the same night. The enumerators were given a specific area to cover, and you can tell from their notebooks which way they walked round. Each family was asked to fill in a form and these were later written up into notebooks. From these notebooks the arithmetical totals were extracted. It is the notebooks which contain the information you want.

These available census records are in the care of the Public Record Office at the Land Registry Office, Portugal Street in London, (see map on p. 54). It is very close to St Catherine's House so that you can often combine visits to both, but it is often more efficient to look at these records elsewhere.

The records were being used so much that they were microfilmed to preserve them and copies of the microfilms were offered to libraries throughout the country. Most towns bought the census films for their own area, and it is much easier to use them there if possible. For instance if you live in Leeds then you can see the census returns on microfilm for the whole of Yorkshire in the Leeds Reference Library. It would not make sense to go to see them in London if your family were from Yorkshire. But if your family were from Cornwall and you lived in Leeds then it would be easier for you to go to London to see the records for Cornwall than to go to (say) Exeter.

The local holdings of census microfilms are always to be preferred to those in London if you can reach them as easily, because so many people use the ones in London. At a local holding in a library they may ask you to book in advance, because they may not have many microfilm readers. It is as well to check on this point before making the journey. The microfilms are usually in the main reference library for the area. Sometimes quite small libraries have them too.

The census records are not only used by family historians, but also by people interested in the history of their street, their village, their town, and so on.

Your greatest problem will be to locate your family, and this is where the information gained from other sources comes in. If you have a birth, marriage, or death certificate, or a will or any other kind of record giving an address, for a year near to one of the census years, then that address may well be the one where your family were residing at the time of the census itself. If, unfortunately, they are not at that address when you find it on the microfilm then they may be nearby, or some clue may indicate where you should look next.

Many Family History Societies are spending time preparing indexes of the census for their area, and the census they usually use for this work is the 1851. It is worth making enquiries to see if such an index is in existence for it can save you hours of searching through a microfilm. For some towns and cities there is a street index in the rooms at Portugal Street, and they also have some of the indexes which are being produced by Family History Societies. If you decide to look at the census there, it is worth checking to see if the area which interests you is covered by one of these indexes.

IF AT ALL POSSIBLE, YOU SHOULD AIM AT FINDING THE ENTRIES FOR YOUR FAMILY IN EACH OF THE CENSUSES FROM THE 1841 TO THE 1881.

As the statistical details were extracted from the notebooks, they were often ticked off by diagonal strokes, and this may make reading some entries very difficult. Although the handwriting in the notebooks is generally good, it is sometimes poor; sometimes the filming is not as good as it might be – so reading the microfilms can present problems at times, apart from the general problem that they are trying for the eyes.

Although the 1841 census is the earliest, it is not the most useful; from the family historian's point of view it has several disadvantages when compared with the later censuses.

The first name given for a household is always that of the head of the household. This name is followed by the names of the other members of the household. In the 1841 census these other members were not asked to state their relationship to the head, but this question was asked in subsequent censuses. It is normally possible to tell who was the wife and who were the children (if the head of the household was a man), but difficult to know exactly, for instance, who was a mother-in-law, an aunt, a niece, a visitor, a brother-in-law, a servant, or any of the other relationships commonly found.

The 1841 is the most difficult to read of the censuses. It was requested that the age of children up to the age of sixteen years be given exactly, but the age of older people was to be rounded down to the nearest five years, i.e., someone aged twenty-one was given as twenty, aged twenty-nine as twenty-five, etc. In later censuses it was requested that people give their *exact* ages – though our ancestors didn't always do as they were asked! For instance, if a wife was older than her husband she would often knock off a year or ten!

The biggest disadvantage of the 1841 census is that people were not asked to state exactly where they were born. Instead of being given a bridge back into the more difficult earlier records, you are only told whether or not your ancestor came from the county in which he was then living, and, on a larger scale, whether he came from the country he was living in or from another within the British Isles – or from a foreign country.

Therefore, although the 1841 is invaluable, of course, it is not as useful as the 1851 and subsequent censuses.

You will find that if your ancestor was a farmer, he will have stated how many acres he farmed, and how many men he employed on a regular basis. If he was in any other trade it is still usual to find stated the number of men employed.

You will find many strange occupations given. If someone says they were 'out of place' this means they were a domestic living-in servant temporarily out of work. If an annuitant, then they had money invested which gave them an income each year for life, the payments normally dying with them. As there were no old-age pensions and no welfare state, people would invest their savings by buying an annuity – this can still be done today. Often a rich woman would give her child into the care of a poor family for the first year or more of its life, to be breast-fed by the woman taking care of it. This accounts for infants 'at nurse'.

A 'cordwainer' was a shoemaker – the name is believed to come from Cordova leather. A 'translator' is also a shoemaker, but instead of new materials he used second-hand ones.

You will find relatives that you didn't know you had, and may be able to find out what became of them later. If you do the ideal thing, and locate your family in each of the censuses, you can then really see the way it developed over the years.

The arrangement of the census may puzzle you at first, but it becomes clearer when you realize that you are looking at photographed books. Each one has several introductory pages telling you just which area is covered; often there is an example of how the forms ought to be filled in – these examples are in the most beautiful handwriting. Then come pages of statistics and, finally, the forms themselves. The notebooks were numbered on the right-hand page. When one area had been covered a new notebook was started, so the introductory pages occur again.

When you find the entry you require, copy it *all* (see example on p.71), taking care to make a note of which census it is taken from, which town or village, and all the details it gives you. It is surprisingly easy in your excitement at finding new information to omit something vital. It is sometimes possible to buy printouts of pages of the census; this can be a great help. If you are consulting the census at a place where they do not have any such facilities, then you can apply by post to the Land Registry Office for printouts, giving the numbers of the reel and the folio.

For the 1841 census the reference number might be something like this: TO 315/2248 Book 1 folio 4; for the 1861 it would be like this: RG 9/ 2248 folio 179 page 4. For 1871, RG 10 is the prefix.

As you look at the microfilm of the census you will notice that in certain places people might be referred to by their initials only. Workhouses, prisons and lunatic asylums are such places, where no doubt it was felt that even after a hundred years of secrecy families would not wish to have the truth about their members revealed. However, it is often possible to identify people if you know, for example, their initials and where they were born and have a suspicion that they may have been living in one of these institutions. A death certificate may give you a place of residence which turns out to be a private nursing home for the mentally ill, for instance. We must not forget that many mental illnesses which are easily cured or controlled today were hopeless only a few decades ago, just as our ancestors died from diseases which can now be cured or prevented.

The Census Enumerators' Notebooks are arranged in columns. For the 1851 and subsequent censuses, reading from left to right, these are:

1. A column with the number on the schedule (this is *not* a house number).
2. A column with the address. In a village this may be vague and difficult to place, while in a town you may be lucky and get both house number and street name.
3. Name and surname of each person. The top one is always the head of the household, who may be either a man or a woman, according to circumstances.
4. Relation to head of household. Sometimes this is confusing. In one particular household I checked on, where the father was away from home, the eldest daughter entered herself as head, then entered her

RESEARCH CHART – CENSUS RETURNS

Year __1851__   Census ref. no. ___HO 123/4567 folio 89 page 10___

Parish/Borough __HORNCHURCH – TOWN WARD NORTH__

County __ESSEX__

Address	Name	Rel. to Head	Con.	Age	Occupation	Where Born	Blind etc.
BUTTS GREEN	CHARLES SMITH	HEAD	MAR	33	LABOURER	SOMERSET BRISTOL	
	MARY "	WIFE	MAR	32	LAUNDRESS	ESSEX HORNCHURCH	
	WILLIAM "	SON		10	SCHOLAR	" "	
	ELIZA "	DAUR		7		" "	DUMB

Example

71

younger sisters as 'daughters'! No doubt the poor girl did not know quite what to put in the circumstances. But as you will be using the census together with other records and other census years, errors like this should not fox you for long.

5. Condition. This means married, unmarried, widow, widower.

6. Age last birthday. This should be exact – apart from any little white lies!

7. Rank, profession or occupation. This is where you find those delightful names of trades which are obsolete today.

8. Where born. This is perhaps the most useful of all the columns.

9. Whether blind, dumb or idiot, etc.

Sometimes the enumerator makes an error which you can unravel. For instance, a York enumerator put down Tockwith, the name of a village near York, when the man was actually born in Stockwith, in Lincolnshire or Nottinghamshire (West and East Stockwith are on the opposite banks of the Trent) – a natural mistake.

In the last column people were required to say if any members of the family were deaf and dumb, blind, imbecile or idiot, or lunatics. One enumerator in the 1871 census has left on record the fact that on the forms he collected (and then wrote up into his notebooks) many persons having little ailments minutely described them, and in one case he had a family returned as 'all healthy' – which he thought was a curious kind of affliction! Another person wrote, 'Mother says I am a luny, but I don't think I am.'

Scotland

In Scotland, the census records are at New Register House, in the same building as the civil registration records. You must book to see the census records, and it would be advisable when possible to visit during the quieter, winter months. (This advice really applies to all visits to places where records are kept; so many people use part of their holidays to carry out research into their families, usually in the better weather, that places much in demand are extra busy then.) Records are available for the censuses of 1841 to 1891, for some reason being released for use by the general public more quickly than in England. Basically the remarks on census returns in England and Wales also apply to Scotland.

It is also possible to request details from the census by post, if you are sure of the address of your family in a census year.

Ireland

The first census was taken in 1821. Obviously Irish people who emigrated to England, Wales or Scotland will appear in the censuses for those countries, after the year of their emigration. Often they will only give their place of origin as 'Ireland' but frequently they do name the town or village as well. Records for the time before the separation of the country, 1922, will all be in Dublin; records after that date will be either in Dublin or Belfast, depending on where your ancestors lived.

Once you have ascertained when they left Ireland, you will want to trace their earlier history in the Irish records. Unfortunately, most of the census records for Ireland for 1821, 1831, 1841 and 1851 were destroyed by fire in 1922 during the Troubles, only a very few remaining. The detailed census records for 1861 to 1891 were not preserved by the authorities.

However, the census returns of 1901 and 1911 are available and may be consulted at the Public Record Office, The Four Courts, Dublin 7, Republic of Ireland. Include a stamped addressed envelope with an international reply coupon, which you can buy at a post office, when writing with an enquiry to the Republic of Ireland.

The Public Record Office cannot carry out searches for you, so unless you can pay a visit you may have to ask the Genealogical Office, Dublin Castle, Dublin 2, Republic of Ireland, to help you. They have a fixed scale of fees for searches.

These censuses cover both Eire and Ulster – Southern and Northern Ireland. They are very similar to the censuses for England and Wales, but more information is given about the houses the families lived in, their religion, whether they spoke Irish or English, and if they were literate.

To fill the gaps of the missing censuses, you may find the Primary Valuation helpful for the 1850s and 1860s. This was carried out between 1847 and 1865 for taxation purposes and is also at the Public Record Office. There is a Valuation Book for each Poor Law Union, giving the names of occupiers of land and buildings.

There were also Tithe Applotment Books compiled between 1823 and 1837, each book covering a parish. Without a clear idea of the family's place of origin it would hardly be practical to try to search either these or the Primary Valuations.

Isle of Man

The censuses for the Isle of Man from 1821 to 1871 are in the care of The Archivist, The Manx Museum and National Trust, Douglas, Isle of Man. 1821 was the first census.

The census for 1841 is incomplete. The censuses dating after 1871 are in the care of the Public Record Office in London in the same way as the English and Welsh censuses; 1881 is available at Portugal Street.

Channel Islands

The Channel Islands are included in the census for England and Wales, and the records are therefore with the other available censuses at the Public Record Office's Land Registry Building in Portugal Street, London. If you are holidaying in the Channel Islands and wish to search for your ancestors while you are there, there are microfilmed copies of the census for Guernsey and the smaller islands (where taken) in Guernsey, and for Jersey in Jersey.

INTERNATIONAL
GENEALOGICAL INDEX

Once you get back to about 1875, this index is available to help you. It is produced by the Church of Jesus Christ of Latter-day Saints, who will be referred to here for the sake of brevity as the Mormons. The Mormons have religious reasons for wishing to identify their ancestors and, in order to help members of their Church to trace their own families, are carrying out a tremendous programme of microfilming records whenever permission is obtained to do so.

The Mormons share the results of their work with the rest of the world, and the International Genealogical Index, or I.G.I., is one of the ways of doing this.

The I.G.I. is an index to information stored in the vast computer at Salt Lake City, and is updated at intervals. It is not a complete or a primary source, but it is extremely useful as a *finding guide*, and is even more useful for the earlier period – before 1837 – where the other great indexes (of civil registration and wills) are not there to help you.

The I.G.I. is available on microfiche; a microfiche, often called fiche for short, is an object about the size of a postcard made of a substance like negative film. These fiches are arranged by country and county, for example, England, Middlesex, and then within that county they are arranged alphabetically by name. This grouping is not strictly alphabetical, since all variants and different spellings of a name will be together, but these groups of names are arranged alphabetically in relation to other groups. You should still be careful in case a variation of your name has got itself separated from the other variants. Within each name the individual Christian names are also alphabetical, and arranged chronologically.

Many reference libraries, archive offices, and individual Family History Societies have bought copies of the I.G.I. for their own areas, usually their own county, so if you live in the same area as your ancestors you should be able to consult a copy easily. Sometimes you may find that a complete set has been bought for the whole *country*. If you wish to refer to the I.G.I. for a distant county, and the local library or society has not bought the copies you want, then you may find that one of the Mormon Branch Libraries (called Stake Libraries) is near you and has a complete set. They are open to the public at certain times and are free, though a donation is welcomed.

Microfiche is being used for so many different purposes now that you may find that you are familiar with handling it, but, if not, it is very simple. At the top of the fiche there is enough information for you to be able to select the right one from the folder in which they are stored – you look for the initial of the surname you are checking on. The fiche is then inserted between the two glass plates of the microfiche reader, and these are gently pushed into the reader, which looks like a television screen. The words which are minutely written on the fiche are then thrown up at a readable size on the screen. To find the bit you want you move the handle of the glass plates holding the fiche.

It is often possible to buy printouts of the microfiche, which costs very little. Sometimes these show just one frame of twenty-five names, sometimes they show a good deal more, and the print can be rather small to read easily. It is very useful to have these printouts to study at your leisure at home, but there will be a great many printouts for a name which frequently occurs. With a less common name it is economic to buy printouts; often you can do this without actually looking at the fiche at all. Some libraries and archive offices and societies, and also the Mormon Church, will sell you printouts by post at prices which vary considerably but are never expensive. You can enquire first how many printouts would be needed to give all the entries for your name for the county which interests you, and then decide whether to buy them all or not. You could always specify, for instance, all the Samuels, or all the Marmadukes, if that was a handed-down Christian name and there were too many of the entire name for you to purchase.

Do not regard the I.G.I. as the answer to all your problems. It is, I repeat, a *finding aid* and if you find an entry which you are sure gives the information for which you have been looking, then you should go where it points, to the original record. The original record will give you fuller information, and you need every scrap of information you can find.

There is also the point that, as deaths are not often entered on the microfiche, you may be merrily working out your descent from a person who died at the age of two.

As the I.G.I. is being constantly updated, it is becoming more and more useful; at the same time, more and more confusing for names which occur frequently. Buy a printout and puzzle it out at home in the winter evenings.

The main columns on the fiche show the following: the surname, the Christian name, the names of the parents or the name of the spouse of the individual, the type of event the entry refers to, the date of the event and the place where it occurred.

The Mormons publish a book called the *Parish and Vital Records Listing*, which should be available in any of their libraries, and which will tell you which parishes in the county you are interested in have had their records fed into the computer in Salt Lake City,

IGI – example

COUNTRY: ENGLAND	COUNTY: ESSEX			AS OF APR 1984
SEX: M- MALE, F- FEMALE, H- HUSBAND, W- WIFE				
NAME	FATHER, MOTHER OR SPOUSE		EVENT DATE	TOWN, PARISH
GREEN, ANN	BILL BLOGGS	W M	23 FEB 1836	WIDFORD
GREEN, JOHN	JAMES GREEN / ALICE	M C	07 AUG 1856	ROXWELL

A - ADULT CHRISTENING, B- BIRTH, C- CHRISTENING,
D - DEATH OR BURIAL, F - BIRTH OR CHRISTENING
OF FIRST KNOWN CHILD, M- MARRIAGE,
N - CENSUS, W - WILL

and which of these have not yet appeared on the I.G.I. microfiche.

The latest to be published is the 1984 I.G.I. It is much larger than the previous issue – for Scotland, for instance, there are 199 extra fiche. The 1984 issue has added 22 million extra names, as a whole, to the previous one.

The Mormon name extraction programme goes up to 1875 as the most recent date, but you may find some entries later than that on the fiche. These have been entered by individual members of the Mormon Church, and may be for dates as late as 1900. A mark like this: @ at a marriage entry indicates that there may be relatives named in the original register. An 'hache' mark after a name indicates extra names in the register entry.

CHURCH RECORDS

By the time you have got back to 1875, if you find an entry in the I.G.I. for one of your family events with a reference to the church where it took place, it begins to be feasible to use church records. Do not go rushing off to the church. More than likely, the records will have been deposited in a record office or other approved depository. Look in the telephone book for the area (most large reference libraries and post offices have a set for the whole country) and find out which local authority covers it, then contact their archivist or record office and ask if they have the registers of the church or chapel you are interested in. If they have and it is possible for you to visit, then do so. It will be a valuable introduction for you to the place and the staff and if there are shelves with books such as directories which you can browse through while you are there, then all the better.

Church of England registers throughout our period are in printed form, filled in by the clergyman, and the type of information given is standard. There are two things to remember, about baptism and burials. What you are looking up in a church register is not the actual event of birth or death, but the religious event of baptism or burial. Baptism can take place at any age and not necessarily at the place where the person was born. Burials are obviously not as variable as far as *time* is concerned, but people are often taken from the *place* where they die to be buried elsewhere. So the information is different in essence from that given by a birth or death certificate. In the case of marriages, the religious celebration and the civil registration of the event usually coincide.

There is no *need* for you to go to use the original

church or chapel records like this, even if you do find the entry in the I.G.I. You can still buy a certificate, and with the information of place supplied by the I.G.I. you should be able to write direct to the local registrar without using the resources of St Catherine's House.

Baptisms
Church of England baptismal registers from 1837 are printed, eight entries to the page, the pages being numbered and the entries also having printed numbers. Information given is: when baptised; child's Christian name; parents' names; their abode; the father's quality, trade or profession; by whom the ceremony was performed.

Recent registers also give alleged date of birth and godparents' names. Entries and pages are still numbered but there are now nine to the page.

It will be seen that a baptismal entry is not as helpful to you as a birth certificate for the purposes of tracing your family. Birth certificates give the place the child was born (which may not be the abode of the parents) and always give the date of birth. They also give the mother's former name, which is often the only bit of information you want from a record of birth. The only information they do *not* give you is the religious information. This is of course very important to your picture of the family, but you can investigate it after the main framework is known.

Marriages
Church of England marriage registers of 1837 and subsequently have two entries to the page. The pages have printed numbers, as does each entry.

The information given is virtually the same as on a marriage certificate, so if it is easy for you to see the register you could save the cost of the certificate and not lose anything. But marriages can be very difficult to find in church records as they often take place in the bride's parish and you probably do not know where that is. Or both bride and groom may be working away from home and marry at their place of residence. In the case of marriages it is usually better to look for the marriage certificate.

Burials

Church of England burial registers give you the following information: name; abode; when buried; age; by whom the ceremony was performed.

This is not as informative as a death certificate, which gives you cause of death and the name of the informant. The informant may well be a relative, which is useful extra information. In any case the death certificate will give you a far better picture of the event than the burial register will.

OTHER SOURCES

Newspapers

Nowadays most people put announcements of births, marriages and deaths in the newspaper, a practice widespread since 1881. The earlier you go – and newspapers go back a surprisingly long way – the fewer such notices become. Copies of old newspapers are sometimes kept in newspaper offices, and often they are to be found in reference libraries. Occasionally you might find that an index has been compiled or is being compiled, but this may only be for certain items on a selective basis. When the paper becomes too fragile to stand much handling, newspapers are often microfilmed.

If you do not live near your family's place of origin but can visit the British Library Newspaper Library at Colindale Avenue, London NW9 5HE, opposite the Colindale tube station (on the Northern Line), old newspapers can be seen there, for the whole of the period we are discussing in this book and, in fact, back to 1801. There is a reading room for the public and the newspapers are from London, the provinces of England, Scotland and Ireland, and also from the Commonwealth and some foreign countries. They can supply you with a photocopy of any item of interest which you find. There is a small car park and a refreshment room with vending machines for drinks and snacks. The library is open every day from 10 a.m. to 5 p.m., except Sundays and some bank holidays, but closed annually for the week after the last complete week in October. People under twenty-one are not normally admitted. To find out more details write to the Superintendent, or ring 01-200 5515.

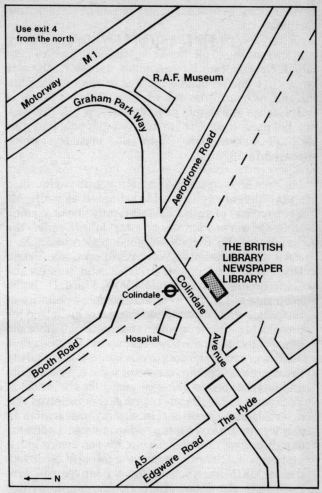

Use exit 4
from the north

M1
Motorway

Graham Park Way

R.A.F. Museum

Aerodrome Road

THE BRITISH
LIBRARY
NEWSPAPER
LIBRARY

Colindale

Colindale Avenue

Hospital

Booth Road

The Hyde

A5 Edgware Road

← N

Unfortunately, newspapers, while fascinating, are great time-wasters. You may find yourself reading them for hours without getting any farther with the history of your family. But they will give you an

85

unrivalled sense of what it was like to be alive at that particular time.

As far as specific help from newspapers goes, if you are not sure, for instance, which of two cousins called George Smith was your ancestor, then to know that one is 'beloved father of May and Nellie' will sort him out from one who was 'beloved father of Ted, George and Annie'. An obituary, if you find one, can be pure gold. Where else would you find this kind of information (from an obituary which appeared in 1928)?

Mr Fred Brunyee age 71 was a potato commission agent at Railway Dock. He collapsed at work. Mr Brunyee was of an old Eastoft family and on coming to Goole worked for the late Mr John Bennet, the founder of the Bennet Steamship Company, as a clerk. He represented West Ward on Goole Urban District in 1894, again in 1922, and was on the Goole Board of Guardians for West Ward. He had a keen interest in farming and made a speciality of the potato and pea sections. For years he helped his brother Mr Wm Brunyee in the management of the family farm at Boothferry and up to the time of his death worked in the potato market at Goole. During the war he was potato inspector for the West Riding and later he became the inspector for the whole of Yorkshire. Quiet and retiring, he collected for hospitals and charities. He was a Conservative in politics. Mr Brunyee left a widow, two sons and four daughters, all married. Two of his sons were killed in the war. Family mourners; Mrs A Brunyee, widow; Mr H Brunyee, son; Mr W Brunyee, son; Mrs C Norman, daughter; Mrs G Denby, daughter; Mrs R Wormald, daughter; Mrs D Dawson, daughter; Miss I Denby, grand-daughter; Mr S Denby, grandson; Mr F Norman, grandson; Miss L Norman, grand-daughter; Mr C Norman, son-in-law;

Mr G Denby, son-in-law; Mr R Wormald, son-in-law; Mr D Dawson, son-in-law; Mrs W Brunyee, daughter-in-law; Mrs W Everett, sister; Mr J B Everett, nephew; Mr H Brunyee, nephew; Mr A Brunyee, nephew; Mrs Kitchen, sister-in-law; Mr W Collier, nephew.

You will notice that an obituary like this tells us about things which have happened throughout a person's life. One important thing to remember in family history is that to find out an *early* piece of information one often has to look at *later* records. This piece of information published after Mr Frederick Brunyee's death tells us when he was born, and the village his family lived in, the initial of his wife, the number and sex of their children and the surnames of the men their daughters married; also that some of those daughters had children, and their names. It does not appear from this obituary as though his sons had children, though other evidence would be needed to check that. It might be that they had emigrated or for some other reason were not able to attend the funeral. We also form a clear picture of his life's work, his character and his interests.

Other newspaper items of interest might include a Golden Wedding, a hundredth birthday, a bankruptcy, a retirement, and many more.

Australians often find vital information in the British newspapers, if their ancestors were transported. If the date of transportation is known and the Assize Court which ordered it, the newspaper write-up of the case is normally the best source of information, for the court records are often very brief indeed.

It is often possible to obtain a photocopy of an item of interest in a newspaper. If for some reason this is not practical, then you can always copy it out.

Records of the Armed Forces

1939–45

The 1939–45 war is, after all, forty years away from us;
people who are grandparents now may have no
memory of it, though to those of us who do remember,
it must surely be the 'great divide' in our lives. Many
younger people who wish to trace their families and
whose parents fought in that war and are now dead,
will need to find information. These records are so
many and split into so many different parts that you
should really read some of the specialist books on the
subject if you want to use them. Only brief hints can be
given here.

Apart from the members of the armed forces, there
was more movement of the civilian population than in
normal times. Women went into the Land Army and
men were Bevin Boys and went down the mines;
children were often separated from their parents and
evacuated to safer areas. Bombing often rendered
people homeless and they had to find somewhere else
to live.

It is worth mentioning again that no census was
taken in 1941, which will be a sad loss to family
historians and other historians in the next century.

Nevertheless, the population clung to 'home' as
much as they could and returned to their original
homes as soon as possible when the disruption was
over.

Many of the records of the 1939–45 war are still
regarded as secret but some are available and many
books have been written about the contribution of
different sections of the Armed Forces. The War
Graves Commission may be helpful if someone died
abroad (see address in next paragraph).

1914–18

This conflict left its memorials on every village green
in the land, sad lists giving the names of young men

lost, often with an added, much shorter list from the Second World War. If a man is known to have died abroad in the wars, the War Graves Commission can be extremely helpful. They can tell you where the grave is, if it is known, and even supply a photograph of it. Their address is:

Commonwealth War Graves Commission
2 Marlow Road
Maidenhead
Berkshire SL6 7DY

They have an alphabetical index by surname giving details of graves or memorials, but when writing to them you should give all the details you can, such as full name, home, Forces rank and number and regiment or section, and so on.

Many medals survive in families, and round the edge of some of those issued is engraved the name and number of the person to whom the medal was awarded. Many families still have service papers, or the bronze plaques issued to the families of men who died. The service number and name of regiment are the most important aids in discovering a war record. Service papers are often so informative that the biography of a man could be written from those alone; they give a personal description, place of birth, trade, medals won, and other information depending on the period.

Earlier wars
The principal wars were the Boer War in South Africa, 1899–1902, and the Crimean War, 1854–56.

The essential difference between the First and Second World Wars and these earlier wars is that the earlier wars were fought by armies of volunteers only and not conscripted men. Many lads joined up for adventure and to see the world; others because they could not find work in civilian life or to escape the consequences of something they had done. Ordinary soldiers and sailors were often looked down on by the civilian population. Officers were different as they were pursuing an expensive career and socially were very well thought of.

The best source for war records is the Public Record Office at Kew, which is not an easy place for beginners. After you have been tracing your family for a while and want to know more about an ancestor's war service, venture there.

However, regiments keep their own records and can often be very helpful.

A good example of the importance of small details is the experience of Mrs Linda Haywood who wished to discover more about her grandmother's war service in the 1914–18 war. All she knew from family tradition was that Mabel Alice Dunford had been firstly in work on munitions, and then had joined the 'Women's Army' and had served at some time in Rouen, France, in the 'stores'.

At first Linda wrote to the Army Records Centre (Ministry of Defence, Bourne Avenue, Hayes, Middlesex UB3 1RF) giving her grandmother's name and enclosing a letter from Mabel's next of kin giving permission for information to be given to Linda. The reply was that nothing could be found, that due to enemy air action in 1940 many records of army personnel who served in 1914–18 had been destroyed and it was probable that M A Dunford's records were amongst them. It was suggested that Linda write to the Army Medal Office (Worcester Road, Droitwich, Worcestershire), who might be able to supply limited information from the Medal Rolls. However, the Army Medal Office later replied that they, too, could find nothing.

Linda's aunt had an autograph book which had belonged to Mabel Alice Dunford at the time she served in France and which had been signed by many friends just before they returned to 'civvies'. One page had been written out to resemble an official pass, allowing Mabel Alice to be 'absent from her quarters for the purpose of proceeding for recreation'. Linda noticed that on this imitation pass the name had been written as Durnford instead of Dunford, and that there was a number, rank, date, and '5th. HRS Rouen'. At the time Linda did not take much notice of these details, but she sent a photocopy of the page to the Curator of the WRAC Museum, Guildford, hoping for background information concerning the type of work carried out by women in France at that time, and asking, what the initials 'HRS' meant.

She learned from the very helpful reply that HRS meant Heavy Repair Shop and it was suggested that she might write to the curator of the Regimental Museum of the Royal Corps of Transport, as the Army Service Corps (as it had been) was responsible for HRSs. Linda was also told that her grandmother would have been entitled to two medals if she was overseas during the war.

Writing once more to the Army Medal Office, Linda quoted the name given on the imitation pass in the autograph book, Durnford, and the number and rank also given there. This time the Army Medal Office found details, under this misspelling, and were able to tell Linda that her grandmother had enlisted on 27 September 1918, as 49545 Worker Mabel Durnford, QMAAC, and had been discharged on 2 November 1919, as medically unfit. She had earned entitlement to the Silver War Badge, the British War Medal and the Victory War Medal. The curator of the Royal Corps of Transport, with this further information, was able to tell Linda that he had a photograph album full of pictures of the 5th HRS at Deville-les-Rouen, and she was able to have a photocopy of a photograph of the stores where her grandmother had worked.

With Apologies...

"Memory prefers to docket happiness, and does not care to keep lasting record of pain."

Pass.

Regiment A.M.Q.A.C.

No. 49545. Rank. Wkr. Name. Dunnford M. ....

has permission to be absent from her quarters from

.... to ....

for the purpose of proceeding to for. Recreation ...

Rouen.

Date. 2.9.19.

Wishing you the very best of
"Health & Happiness" on your
return to "Civvies"

yours sincerely
Marion Jarrow)
5th M.N.S.
Rouen.

....
Unit Administrator.

.... Camp.

September 1919.

The 'Women's Army' was first known as the Women's Army Auxiliary Corps (WAAC) but after April 1918 it became the Queen Mary's Army Auxiliary Corps (QMAAC). Linda has a photograph of her grandmother in uniform.

This shows how important tiny details are, how a small difference in a surname can stop one finding the information, and how care and persistence often pay off. Mabel Alice's surname must have been misspelled when she enlisted, and stayed misspelled for the duration of her war service.

Another instance of success in tracing details of an army career is that of Mrs Freda Foster, who found that her grandfather was in the Household Cavalry. His marriage certificate of 1902 told her that he was stationed at Knightsbridge Barracks at that time, and was then twenty-four years old. The Household Cavalry Museum at Combermere Barracks, Windsor, Berks, was able to give Mrs Foster the dates on which he enlisted and was discharged, and the details he had been required to give on enlistment. As he had been in the Household Cavalry when Queen Victoria's funeral procession and also when King Edward VIII's coronation procession took place, she can feel very proud not only of his service in such an illustrious regiment but also that he may well have taken part in those national events.

Both these examples show the importance of knowing which part of the Armed Forces an ancestor has served in, before making enquiries. Tiny clues – such as badges worn in photographs – must be followed up if possible, to identify this, otherwise you are searching for a needle in a haystack. Once you have positive information, the Forces museums and record departments can help you.

Records of Employers

War service records are touched on here because so many members of the general population are involved, and at least some general guidance can be given. Employers, however, vary considerably. Some of them do keep records of former employees. Examples of this are the Post Office and the Railways, but you should have positive information about when and where your ancestor worked before asking them if they can give you further information. Other firms and companies may well also hold records. At least it is worth asking. They can only tell you, at worst, that the records have been destroyed or are unavailable for consultation.

If your ancestor worked for the Post Office, you may glean some information from the Post Office Archives, Freeling House, 23 Glasshill Street, London SE1 0BQ, (tel. 01-261 1145). If your ancestor worked for the Railways, you may possibly find something among the records at the Public Record Office at Kew.

A good many records of police personnel went to aid the Salvage Drive for waste paper during the 1939–45 war.

Public Record Office at Kew

I do not regard the PRO at Kew as a place for beginners; it can be rather frightening with all its space-age technology, even though the staff are so kind and helpful. But for those who wish to venture! . . .

The Public Record Office is in several sections, the first to be established being the beautiful building on Chancery Lane. Another section of the PRO is the Land Registry Office on Portugal Street which was mentioned in the section on the census. Having outgrown the existing accommodation, the PRO fairly recently built the new building at Kew.

Most records of the period covered in this book will be at Kew and not at Chancery Lane. Take a tube to Kew and then walk (see map). The PRO is open on weekdays and an appointment is not needed, but you

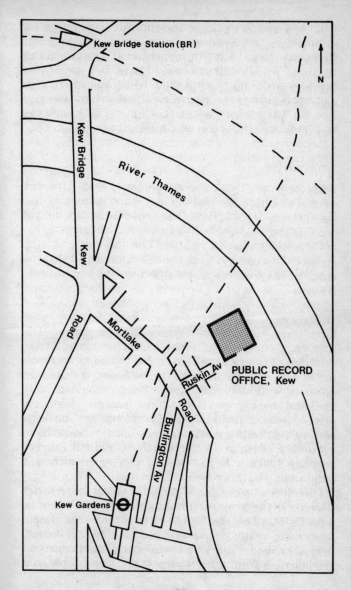

will need a reader's ticket and this must be applied for in advance. (A reader's ticket is also needed for Chancery Lane, but you can look at the census at Portugal Street without one.) There is a small restaurant in the building at Kew which searchers may use. Because it is less convenient than Central London, plan a visit extra carefully. It is possible to buy booklets telling you which records are available.

Directories

Directories are books about places, which give you details of where the place is and what its history has been, the main buildings, the early-closing day, lists of some of the people who live there, and so on.

Directories began about the middle of the eighteenth century, and by the time our period is reached they were well established and voluminous. Kelly is a name we all know in relation to directories, as their editions were regularly published until about 1977. There were many other firms issuing early directories, for example White, Baines, Lamb. The title page often reads 'History, Gazetteer, and Directory' but they are usually referred to simply as directories. Copies for past years can be found in reference libraries and may sometimes be available in secondhand bookshops. Some have recently been reprinted by such firms as David and Charles. The 'local history' section of a good reference library should have a number of them. In London the Guildhall Library and the Library of the Society of Genealogists are outstanding in this respect.

Directories sometimes include street directories which give the names of inhabitants of the town, but as it seems these entries had to be paid for by the people concerned, many people are not included. However, they are a useful check and reinforcement of what you are learning from other sources, and invaluable as a picture of the times. Such details as the places the carrier's cart went to, the frequency of market days and other such information may give you a clue when you are stuck.

Telephone Directories

These are really only useful to those who have very unusual names. In their case it is well worth going through the telephone directories for the entire country and noting where the name occurs. It may be that there are large areas of the country where the surname does not occur at all, other areas where it occurs only a few times, and others again where there are a large number of entries. A complete set of directories is usually to be found in large post offices and in reference libraries. Sometimes family historians contact other people of the same name given in telephone directories either by phone or by letter and this may lead to very useful contacts. If people do not wish to respond they have no need to do so. Even without contacting the people who bear the same name, leafing through the telephone directories can give you a useful idea of the national distribution of your name. This is very valuable information to have.

If your family were early subscribers to the telephone system, you may be helped by referring to the early directories. It is no longer as easy to look at these at it used to be before privatisation of British Telecom. But you can make an appointment to see them on Wednesday afternoons between 1 and 4 p.m. at Telecom Technology Showcase, 135 Queen Victoria Street, London EC4V 4AT, (tel. 01-248 7444). There are also some early telephone directories in the Guildhall Library in London and in the Bodleian Library in Oxford.

Although old telephone directories go back to the 1880s, there are very few of them before the 1940s.

Family Papers

You should not have any difficulty in reading most things dating back to 1837; printed matter is much the same as ours today, and although handwriting was often in a different style it is usually understandable. Any problems with handwriting are most likely due to the carelessness of the writer – just as in our own times!

There are two things you may come across, though, which may surprise you. The first is the custom, particularly prevalent before the introduction of the Penny Post, of 'crossing' writing when writing a letter. This means that when the writer had filled a sheet in the normal manner, they turned the sheet of paper at right angles and continued writing *across* the previous lines – at right angles to them. This means you can spend ages puzzling it out.

The other thing you may well come across is the 'long *s*'. Often people think this is an *f*. Before our period, it was used in printing, but that had died out just about completely by 1837. In handwriting, however, people who had been taught the long *s* in childhood continued to use it, and you will come across it in handwriting as late as 1900, if not later, and it can occur at times on official documents such as birth, marriage and death certificates. It was used mainly where two *s*s come together, and the first was written as a long *s* while the second was written as a normal small *s*. This form of double *s* has a long history; it was part of traditional German handwriting and in the

Antony Nussey Esquire

printed form has been used in Germany until recent times. (They also used the long *s* for an initial, and two long *ss* in the middle of words when preceded by a short vowel.) In Greek also there are two different forms of written and printed *s*. So our English long *s* is in line with European history and use; and you will come across it in the printed form when you delve into earlier periods of your family's history.

Even if you have inherited nothing in the way of family papers, papers which mention your ancestors or once belonged to them may have found their way into record offices somewhere in the country. Some family solicitors have deposited their ancient papers, and these are a wonderful treasure house if they happen to refer to your ancestors. At other times, old families have deposited the contents of their Muniment Rooms, feeling that they would be of use to historians. Some societies such as the Society of Genealogists and various archaeological societies, have received such gifts and so have local authorities. These deposits may contain draft wills, indentures, property and other deeds, birth, marriage and death certificates, litigation papers and family correspondence. It is seldom that anyone has had the time to make proper indexes or catalogues of them, so they can be very time-consuming to look through, but they can be very rewarding, giving you lots of interesting detail to add to your family history.

The Society of Genealogists' document collection started in 1911, built up from donations by members and non-members and by the British Record Association. It is divided into two sections.

1. Collections of all documents relating to one specific family, 11,000 in their 1965 list.

2. Documents relating to several persons or families living in one particular place. Large collections are

Certificate No. 114

HOLLINGBOURN & MALLING RURAL DISTRICT COUNCILS
(AIR RAID PRECAUTIONS)

I certify that Mr. William DIXON

attended a course of anti-gas training at Aylesford, Kent

and qualified in civilian anti-gas precautions in accordance with the instructions laid down by

the Home Office.

MAIDSTONE.

20th March, 1939

P. Andrew

Air Raid Precautions Officer.

mentioned in the 'Family History' section of the card catalogue.

County, town and village histories are very well worth reading. Even if they do not actually mention your ancestor who lived in the place, they will give you an idea of what it was like. The Victoria County Histories, which can be found in good reference libraries, can be very helpful. Have a good look round your reference library, or the reference library in the place from which your family came, and you will find much to interest you ... County and Place name books, books with pedigrees of the aristocratic families in the area – who knows what you might find! Quite often people bring out little histories of their own village or part of a town and these are marvellous sources of information and fascinating to read.

The Poorhouse or Workhouse

If your family went through a bad patch, and had to have help, they might be mentioned in poorhouse and workhouse records, which might survive in record offices or with record societies. The workhouse often acted as a maternity hospital in large towns if a woman's husband was away and there were no female relatives near to help. They also acted as mortuaries; people drowned in the Sheffield Flood of 1864 were taken into the workhouse. Elderly people were taken in for nursing when their families could not cope – though it must be said that it was the dread of working people to end their days in the workhouse. In the period we are covering, life was grim in most workhouses, but humanity must have prevailed in some. Almshouses were not the same at all and seem to have been happy places.

Life and Schools

Mentioning the poorhouse records reminds us how much life has changed.

It is easy to be caught up in the mechanics of tracing your family and to forget that what you are tracing are real human lives, lived through widely varied conditions. The jobs we do are different; in 1851 a third of all the women in London aged between fifteen and twenty-four were in domestic service, and most of them were migrants from the poorer agricultural areas. Including male servants, there were nearly 200,000 domestic servants in London. One has only to read Mrs Beeton's 'Household Management', or any of the less well-known books on how to run a house, to be able to picture fairly accurately the kind of life these servants led.

During the same period, throughout the country the revolution in the means of production was bringing hardship and poverty. Woolcombers in Bradford, formerly the labour aristocrats of the wool trade, saw their wages drop from 24s. a week in the early 1820s to about 6s. a week in the 1850s. Emigration often seemed to be the only answer. Later in the century, in about 1875, the first shiploads of wheat from Canada precipitated a national depression in agriculture from which the country only truly recovered during the 1940–45 war.

Another great change has been in education. Of course, there have always been schools, but it is only since the Education Act of the 1870s that education has become universal and free. Those of our ancestors who could not write probably never had the chance to learn.

In the village of Huntington, a fairly typical village (if anything can be typical), there had been a school since at least 1764, a private school. By 1865, there was a school for the parish kept by the vicar, with twenty-four children out of a child population of sixty in the village. Even after elementary education became compulsory, a 'board school' was not in fact opened until 1877; there was still a charge – indeed, the education provided was not free until 1891.

School log books survive, frequently to be found in their original school or often in the custody of the Local Education Authority. They make fascinating reading!

'25th July 1877. Only very poor attendance in consequence of hay making.'

Going back to 1837 may not seem very far – and of course, I hope that you will have enjoyed your search so much and developed so much expertise that you will be ready to tackle the greater problems of earlier records. But . . . if I, personally, were only to have the period back to 1837, and the records of the place my ancestors came from, there is so much to discover, so much to work out, that I think I could be quite content.

APPENDIX 1

Problems in tracing a family using civil registration in England and Wales

Although in theory it is so easy to trace your family through the civil registration records, in practice there are often difficulties. Thorough preparation – being extra careful to note down every apparently trivial remark your relatives make about the family – can save what looks like a lost cause. At other times slight variations may throw you off the scent. For example:

a) If a child was named John Henry, he may have been registered as Henry John.

b) If he was born before his parents' marriage, he may have been registered under his mother's maiden name, or if his mother married twice the child might later have been known by the surname of the second husband and not by that of his father.

c) If his name was not decided at the time of registration, he may have been registered simply as 'male'.

d) His surname may have ben slightly misspelt by the original registrar, or a copying mistake may have been made when completing the return to send to the Registrar General, or by the Registrar General's office staff when recopying the entry. It is surprising how a misread letter can prevent an entry being found.

One lady ordered a certificate of birth and found that her ancestor's mother's maiden name was given as

'Lowland'. She searched for the Lowland family for some years with no success at all. Then, as a last hope, she ordered the birth certificate of another child of the same family, and on that certificate the mother's maiden name was given as 'Roland'. She was able to trace the Roland family back with no further trouble. Perhaps the registrar had misheard the name on the first occasion!

In another case, after careful searching in the indexes at St Catherine's, a marriage certificate could not be found for a man whose surname was Sewter. At last a chance was taken and the marriage certificate for his bride's name was ordered. When it came, the bridegroom's name was given as Senter, or perhaps Serter – it was impossible to tell which. Puzzled by the discrepancy, the local registrar's office, where the marriage had originally been registered, was approached. There it was confirmed that the bridegroom had signed his name on the original entry as Sewter.

Don't forget how recently universal education came in; before that, people did not bother much about correct spelling, and final *e*s or *s*s meant nothing. A phonetic spelling may stop you recognising your own surname. An initial *h*, if dropped, would put the name in a different part of the alphabet! Mackson and Magson and Maxson might fox you; Orwell or Horwel.

Sometimes people don't like their Christian names or are known by a nickname. Mary is often called Polly, and Frances, Fanny; Martha is Patty; Ellen is Nelly.

Another difficulty is when there are many entries, say for William Smith. If you know that William had a brother called Nathaniel Smith then you may be able to find *him* more easily and as long as they were full brothers – i.e., from the same marriage – then you will gain the same information about parents from Nathaniel's birth certificate as you would from Bill's.

It is surprising how vague people can be about their age! Bear that in mind. But, oddly enough, they usually give the right day and month of birth.

Births had to be registered within six weeks, so although you may be sure you are working on the right date, the birth might be registered in the next quarter. Marriages are registered at once, and death certificates would only be delayed in the case of an inquest.

Did the event in fact take place in Scotland or Ireland? If so, you will not find it at St Catherine's House.

If you suspect that the event may have occurred abroad, then look at the *Miscellaneous Indexes* which cover the returns made by the British Consuls, *Births and Marriages at Sea, Army Births and Deaths*, etc. In the case of India, if you do not find anything in the miscellaneous indexes, try the India Office Library and ask if they can help.

In the first ten years of the system a percentage of births were not registered – 'many thousands', according to the Registrar General in 1844 – and one can understand this when so many babies died soon after birth; it would seem worth waiting to see if in fact the child was going to live. Then, a fine was brought in for non-registration and the percentage improved. Even today, though, one comes across the occasional case of non-registration. This is rare, so do not jump to the conclusion that your ancestor was not registered if you don't find him. It is far more likely that some slight change is preventing you from identifying him.

A few deaths also escaped registration; but people have always been keen on their marriage lines and if you can't find a marriage you may have one of the surnames wrong. A marriage may have been registered but you cannot find it. a) You may not be aware that the bride married twice; you may be looking for her second marriage but under her maiden name. b) You may know what someone's father was called, but not know that he or she was born before their parents' marriage and married under their mother's maiden name. c) If the father died young and the mother remarried, they may have used the step-father's name and married under that. d) If a marriage was childless for many years and then a child arrived, you may be looking for the ceremony years too late. The age of the parents will help here, if you find them in the census.

There are many other possibilities. Addresses can be a source of trouble. They are the address at which the bride and groom were residing at the time of marriage; and if they were married by licence they need only have been at that address for a few days. It is easy to assume that it is the address of the family home. Many people worked away from home and lived at their place of work. Farm labourers lived in; so did many shop assistants.

It is important to keep your family in touch with your progress even if they are not interested. 'How are you getting on with digging up skeletons?' asked my aunt, who was antagonistic to the whole idea. 'I can't find the birth certificate for great-grandfather Richard Hill,' I replied glumly. 'Have you looked under Brunyee?' she asked. I knew that there had been a change of family name, which was the result of a clause in a will, but I had never expected it to be as recent as my great-grandfather, who only died in 1941. On checking, however, I found him straight away, registered as Richard Brunyee. His name was officially changed when he was one year old.

If you are working correctly and using civil registration together with the census and other records, you will find people, one way or another. Finding a family in the census may save you a long search in the civil registration indexes, as you will have a good idea of birth dates and likely marriage dates.

Because you are looking at an index, and compilers are fallible, there is an outside chance that the event was registered and missed from the index.

In cases where, due to the frequent occurrence of a name, you cannot be sure which is the right certificate to order, you may use the 'checking' procedure on a different application form. You select a number of entries and the officials will check each against the 'checking points' you give to them. You are charged for each check made. Either they find which is the right certificate, which is fine, or the form comes back to you marked 'negative'. It is not an altogether satisfactory procedure.

Problems in Scotland
Tracing back to 1837 in Scotland can be a problem because the civil registration system did not begin until 1855. Before that date the only record dealt with in this book is the first useful census, of 1841. However, the parish registers are stored in New Register House, with the census (booking required to see them) and by the time you have worked your way back to that point the later registers should not prove too difficult. The precise details of 'place born' from the 1851 census are very important. There were under a thousand parishes in Scotland. This is not a large number of parishes compared to England, where Yorkshire alone has about seven hundred parishes.

The parish registers are those of the Established Church of Scotland.

Recommended reading for all those with Scottish ancestry is *Scottish Roots*, by Alwyn James, published in 1981 by Macdonald Publishers, Loanhead, Midlothian EH20 9SY (price £3.95).

Irish ancestry is undoubtedly much more difficult to trace than English, Scottish or Welsh (although I would quail at the thought of tracing a Jones in Wales!). The main problem with tracing families who come from Ireland is that in 1922, during the Troubles, an incendiary bomb was thrown into the Inns of Court in Dublin where many records were. Probably as many as two-thirds of the Irish records were destroyed. People interested in Irish families are working hard to try to make it easier to trace them – by discovering other sources of information, such as newspapers, and doing the best with what is available – so it would be a good idea to join the Irish Family History Society and learn from the people who are actively using the records, what can be done.

The Ulster Historical Foundation, which has the same address as the Public Record Office for Northern Ireland (66 Balmoral Avenue, Belfast BT9 6NY), has been carrying out a very valuable programme of research and publication which should be of help to you. There is a registration fee when you ask for their help, and a fee for any searches they may do for you, but compared with the cost of actually visiting Northern Ireland and doing your own research in difficult and unfamiliar records, this should be money well spent. This is one of the few cases where paying for the help of experts is well justified. But see how much you can do on your own first; you will find it very satisfying! And in any case, the experts will want as much information as you can give them to work on.

Problems with the Census

If your family are not at the specific address where you expected to find them, look at the neighbourhood, or nearby villages. Finding other families of the same surname may indicate that this is the family home area.

Age may be inaccurate – younger members of the family may have estimated the age of the elderly.

The birthplace given may be inaccurate, or not that where the person was baptised (if the age takes you back to pre-1837).

Note the other people you find of the same surname, even if you don't find your own family. They may turn out to be related and help you later.

If you don't find your family in the census you are examining, try earlier and later ones for the same place.

Look out for people living in someone else's household – the daughter who is living-in somewhere as a servant; the son who is a live-in apprentice; the old mother or father who is living with a married daughter you didn't know about.

If you find the family, their parents or brothers and sisters may still be living in the village the person has named as their birthplace; have a look in the same census, at that place.

Note the area they are living in, the types of occupations, etc. Note *all* the family occupations. They may give you a lead back, apart from their intrinsic interest.

APPENDIX 2

Civil registration district codes, England and Wales: numbering of districts in the index books

These codes will help you to locate the county in which the registration district lies.

1837–1851 (Roman numerals)

I London and Middlesex
II London and Middlesex
III London and Middlesex
IV London and Surrey
V Kent
VI Beds., Berks., Bucks., and Herts.
VII Hants. and Sussex
VIII Dorset, Hants. and Wilts.
IX Cornwall and Devon
X Devon and Somerset
XI Glos., Soms. and Warwicks.
XII Essex and Suffolk
XIII Norfolk and Suffolk
XIV Cambs., Hunts., and Lincs.
XV Leics., Northants., Notts., and Rutland
XVI Oxon., Staffs., and Warwicks.
XVII Staffs.
XVIII Glos., Salop., Staffs., Warwicks., and Worcs.
XIX Cheshire, Derbys., and Flints.
XX Lancashire
XXI Lancashire and Yorks.
XXII Yorkshire
XXIII Yorkshire
XXIV Durham and Yorkshire
XXV Cumberland, Lancs., Northumberland and Westmorland

XXVI Brecknocks. Carmarthens., Glams., Herefords.,
　　 Mons., Pembs., Radnors. and Salop.
XXVII Anglesey, Caernarvons., Cardigans., Denbighs.,
　　 Flints., Merioneths., and Montgomeryshire

1852–Aug. 1946

1a London and Middlesex
1b London and Middlesex
1c London and Middlesex
1d London, Kent and Surrey
2a Kent and Surrey
2b Hants. and Sussex
2c Berks. and Hants.
3a Berks., Bucks., Herts., Middlx. and Oxon.
3b Beds., Cambs., Hunts., Notts., and Suffolk
4a Essex and Suffolk
4b Norfolk
5a Dorset and Wiltshire
5b Devonshire
5c Cornwall and Somerset
6a Glos., Herefords. and Salop.
6b Staffs., Warwicks. and Worcs.
6c Warwicks. and Worcs.
6d Warwicks.
7a Leics., Lincs. and Rutlands.
7b Derbyshire and Notts.
8a Cheshire
8b Lancashire
8c Lancashire
8d Lancashire
8e Lancashire
9a Yorkshire
9b Yorkshire
9c Yorkshire
9d Yorkshire
10a Durham

10b Cumberland, Northumberland and Westmorland
11a Glamorgan, Monmouth and Pembrokeshire
11b Anglesey, Brecknocks., Denbighs., Flints., Montgomeryshire and Radnorshire

1946 to the present

Arabic numerals with a large letter.

INDEX

The Freakiest, Funniest Book About Animals – *Ever!*

ODDBODS!

Bill Garnett

FIRST THERE WAS *THE NAKED APE*. THEN CAME *THE NAKED NUN* ... NOW – AT LAST – THE NAKED TRUTH!

There are creatures that walk this planet which:

* *Bathe in acid*
* *Baffle Radar*
* *Turn into plants*
* *Do business – and have sex – without their heads*

You'll find them – and many others even stranger – in *ODDBODS!*

IT'S EVERYTHING YOU NEVER WANTED TO KNOW ABOUT ANIMALS – BUT WILL BE STAGGERED TO HEAR!

HUMOUR/NON-FICTION   0 7221 3809 1   £1.75

A selection of bestsellers from SPHERE

FICTION

STREET SONG	Emma Blair	£3.50 ☐
GOLDEN TRIPLE TIME	Zoe Garrison	£2.95 ☐
BEACHES	Iris Rainer Dart	£2.95 ☐
RAINBOW SOLDIERS	Walter Winward	£3.50 ☐
FAMILY ALBUM	Danielle Steel	£2.95 ☐

FILM AND TV TIE-IN

MONA LISA	John Luther Novak	£2.50 ☐
BLOCKBUSTERS GOLD RUN		£1.95 ☐
9½ WEEKS	Elizabeth McNeil	£1.95 ☐
BOON	Anthony Masters	£2.50 ☐
AUF WIEDERSEHEN PET 2	Fred Taylor	£2.75 ☐

NON-FICTION

BURTON: THE MAN BEHIND THE MYTH	Penny Junor	£2.95 ☐
THE DISAPPEARED	John Simpson & Jana Bennett	£4.95 ☐
THE LAST NAZI: THE LIFE AND TIMES OF JOSEPH MENGELE	Gerald Astor	£3.50 ☐
THE FALL OF SAIGON	David Butler	£3.95 ☐
LET'S FACE IT	Christine Piff	£2.50 ☐

All Sphere books are available at your local bookshop or newsagent, or can be ordered direct from the publisher. Just tick the titles you want and fill in the form below.

Name _____

Address _____

_____

Write to Sphere Books, Cash Sales Department, P.O. Box 11, Falmouth, Cornwall TR10 9EN.

Please enclose a cheque or postal order to the value of the cover price plus:

UK: 55p for the first book, 22p for the second book and 14p for each additional book ordered to a maximum charge of £1.75.

OVERSEAS: £1.00 for the first book plus 25p per copy for each additional book.

BFPO & EIRE: 55p for the first book, 22p for the second book plus 14p per copy for the next 7 books, thereafter 8p per book.

Sphere Books reserve the right to show new retail prices on covers which may differ from those previously advertised in the text or elsewhere, and to increase postal rates in accordance with the PO.